Jingle All the Way

40 small stitcheries to make your home merry

DEBBIE BUSBY

C&T PUBLISHING
Another Maker Inspired!

Copyright © 2022 by Debbie Busby

Publisher: Amy Barrett-Daffin

Creative Director: Gailen Runge

Senior Editor: Roxane Cerda

Technical Editor: Elizabeth Tisinger Beese

Copy Editor: Sheila Chapman Ryan

Illustrator: Lisa Lauch

Cover and Interior Designer: Adrienne Smitke

Photographer: Brent Kane

Production Coordinator: Zinnia Heinzmann

Published by C&T Publishing, Inc., P.O. Box 1456, Lafayette, CA 94549

Library of Congress Control Number: 2023932861

Printed in the USA

10 9 8 7 6 5 4 3 2

DEDICATION

To my sisters, Janice, Arlene, and Mary Ann—the three people who have known me from then until now. I can't imagine my life without the three of you around to nudge me forward when need be, to cheer me on along the way, and to celebrate with me the victories in success. Thank you for always being there with me and for me! We are "the Brown girls."

Contents

Introduction

It seems that most of my earliest memories are helped along by old family photos. You know the ones . . . the old black-and-white photos that have been stuffed in old shoe boxes and have bent corners, or the ones that have shuffled their way to the bottom of a drawer. Those are my favorites; those photos display the memories of Christmas that I hold close to my heart. My parents, who always had very little, always seemed to make Christmas special.

And what made the holiday so special was exchanging gifts that were crafted by hand. My dad spent hours, unbeknownst to me and my sisters, building dollhouses and cradles, playpens, toy blocks, toy trains, toy airplanes, and wooden clocks (which taught us girls to tell time).

My mother stitched and sewed into the late hours of the night, making us matching Christmas dresses (which I recall itched like crazy with their scratchy slips and lace). She made us matching pajamas, endless supplies of doll clothes, animal-shaped pillows, and silly stuffed animals. Those are the gifts and memories I remember and cherish.

So it seems only fitting to continue those wonderful handmade traditions and pass on the memories to my children and grandchildren. I hope they cherish handmade gifts and decor—and I hope you do too!

The projects in this book include simple motifs and hand-sewn messages of Christmas cheer using cotton fabric, beautiful wools, hand-dyed linen, rickrack, trims, buttons, bells, a bit of fiberfill stuffing, and of course a needle and thread. My wish is that these designs add some fun to your Christmas stitching and find their way into your Christmas memories.

Happy stitching and merry Christmas wishes!

~ Debbie

Here you'll find basic information about my favorite sewing notions and textiles that I love to use in my stitching.

Tools and Supplies

You have many choices available when choosing fabrics, wools, and notions and embellishments—don't limit yourself to just the ideas in this book. There are always new products on the market and I encourage you to try what's new along with sifting through the things you have on hand. When you have the tools you love to use, it makes each project more fun to create. One of the things that makes these projects so fun is that they don't require many tools—and the tools they do require are easy to take along so you can stitch anywhere. Some of my favorite tools I keep on hand for wool appliqué and embroidery include freezer paper, Glad Press'n Seal, mechanical pencils, several types and sizes of scissors, an iron, different sizes of needles, appliqué pins, and a variety of beautiful threads.

Glad Press'n Seal. I use this grocery store item for transferring embroidery patterns. Press'n Seal has a smooth side and a tacky side. Always use it with the tacky side down. Use a permanent fine-point marker to trace the designs so that ink won't smear or rub off onto your hands or project. If the wool is very dark, it's helpful to use a brightly colored permanent marker, such as silver or bright pink, rather than black.

Freezer paper. Cutting out wool-appliqué shapes is easy with the use of freezer paper, which you can find at most grocery stores. Freezer paper has a dull side and a shiny side; trace appliqué shapes onto the dull side with the shiny side facing down.

Needles. I find myself using embroidery and chenille needles the most in my projects. I choose my needles based on the size of the eye. If I can thread it, I can stitch with it. My favorite embroidery needles are size 8. If you're using a heavier thread, a chenille #22 needle has a large eye and works well. I also like to keep long doll needles in my pincushion, which I use for sewing buttons through thicker bowl fillers and pincushions.

Scissors. It's important to have a nice pair of sharp, pointed scissors when cutting out your wool pieces for wool appliqué. A small pair is handy when you need to cut tiny pieces. They're also great for clipping threads.

Threads. Beautiful pearl cotton, embroidery floss, wool threads, and even quilting threads are fun to sew with. I love to use Valdani 100% cotton solid or variegated pearl cotton, size 12. I also use a single strand of assorted quilting threads and embroidery floss for a finer stitch that doesn't stand out as much for tiny wool pieces. If you want to use six-strand embroidery floss, two strands will look similar to size 12 pearl cotton.

Wool. All the wool used for the projects in this book is 100% wool that has been felted. This is my go-to wool of choice and gives me the best outcome. When choosing wool to appliqué with, it's important to consider the weight of the wool. Wools vary in weight and include flannel, suit weight, and blanket weight. In my experience, flannel-weight wool works best. Suit-weight wools tend to be too lightweight and don't always felt well. Coat weight for appliqué tends to be too heavy.

Wool for appliqué should be felted before use. The process of felting wool causes the fibers of the wool to shrink and tighten, which makes the wool thicker and stops the cut edges from fraying. If you have wool that hasn't been felted, the steps are simple. To felt wool, place the wool in a hot-water wash with agitation and a cold-water rinse. The change of temperature is what helps in the felting of the wool. Follow up by drying the wool on high heat. I like to place a dry towel in the dryer when drying my wool to help absorb the extra moisture for a quicker drying time. Remove the wool from the dryer and lay it out flat to avoid wrinkling.

Wool Appliqué

The simplicity of wool appliqué is what makes it so easy and fun. Because you're using wool that has been felted, the wool can be cut into shapes without the edges raveling, which means there's no need to turn under the edges when appliquéing. I use freezer paper to cut out the appliqué shapes.

1 Place the freezer paper shiny side down over the pattern; you'll be able to see through the freezer paper well enough to trace the shape. Use a pencil or permanent marker so that the ink won't rub off onto your hands or the wool. It's helpful to label the pieces as you trace them so you'll know which wool to use when you get to the ironing board. Leave at least ⅛" of space between traced patterns.

2 Cut out the shapes ⅛" to ¼" from the traced line. *Do not cut on the traced line.*

3 Set the iron to the wool setting. With the shiny side down, iron each freezer-paper shape onto the appropriate wool color. If you're cutting multiple pieces from the same piece of wool, place the shapes close together to maximize the use of the wool.

4 Cut out the appliqué shapes on the traced lines, cutting through the freezer paper and wool at the same time.

5 Remove the freezer paper from the wool before you appliqué. If you have multiple pieces that are similar in shape and size, it's helpful to keep the labeled freezer paper on them until you've positioned everything on the background fabric.

6 Place the background on a flat surface and position the appliqué pieces on it. Pin the pieces in place with appliqué pins, which are short and less likely to catch the thread. My favorites are Clover appliqué pins. To make sure that everything is in its proper place, position all the appliqué pieces on the background for placement before you begin stitching. Then remove the topmost pieces and stitch the bottom layer of appliqués first.

Prevent Fraying

Some of the appliqué pieces are small, and pulling too hard while stitching can distort the shapes, so handle them gently. Use a dab of Dritz Fray Check (a liquid sealant) to keep tiny pieces from fraying.

7 Stitch around the edge of each appliqué to secure it to the background. I use a blanket stitch or whipstitch. The blanket stitch takes a bit more time and uses more thread but gives a great look and outlines the design. The whipstitch is quick and easy and uses less thread. I usually whipstitch small appliqué pieces since it's less bulky. See "Stitch Guide" on page 9 if you're unfamiliar with these stitches.

8 When the appliqué is complete, press the project. Using steam, press from the back first. Turn the piece over and use a pressing cloth or a scrap of cotton on the front to prevent the wool pieces from overheating or scorching.

Embroidery

Here you'll find techniques for transferring embroidery designs to fabric, along with a guide to the embroidery stitches used throughout the book. When transferring embroidery designs onto the fabric, you'll use different techniques depending on the color of the background.

Transferring Embroidery Designs onto Light-Colored Cotton Fabric

To transfer a design onto light-colored cotton fabric, use a light box or window.

1 Lay the embroidery pattern on the light box or secure it to the window with painter's tape.

2 Position and tape the fabric over the pattern. Trace the design very lightly with a pencil or water-soluble marker. You could also use a Pilot FriXion pen (my preference), which disappears with the heat of an iron.

Skip the Hoop

Since these projects are so small, I don't think it's necessary to use an embroidery hoop when embroidering.

Transferring Embroidery Designs onto Dark-Colored Cotton Fabric

To transfer a design onto dark-colored cotton fabric or heavier fabric such as wool, I use Glad Press'n Seal.

1 Cut a piece of Press'n Seal large enough to cover the embroidery design or appliqué shape. With the tacky side down, carefully lay the Press'n Seal over the pattern and smooth out any wrinkles. Use a permanent marker to trace the pattern directly onto the smooth side of the Press'n Seal.

2 After the ink has dried, lift the marked Press'n Seal and position it on the fabric, pressing it and smoothing out any wrinkles with your hands. The Press'n Seal will stay in place on its own. Trim away any excess that extends beyond the edges of the fabric.

3 Embroider the design, stitching through the Press'n Seal. For best results, make the stitches more taut than you normally would because removing the plastic will exert tension on the stitching. If the pattern includes lazy daisy stitches, it's best to wait until you've removed the Press'n Seal to make them. (Because the lazy daisy stitches are a bit loose, they can easily become distorted as you remove the Press'n Seal.)

4 When you've finished the embroidery, carefully peel away the Press'n Seal from the fabric and stitches. Use a small pair of tweezers to remove any bits of plastic wrap that remain.

Stitch Guide

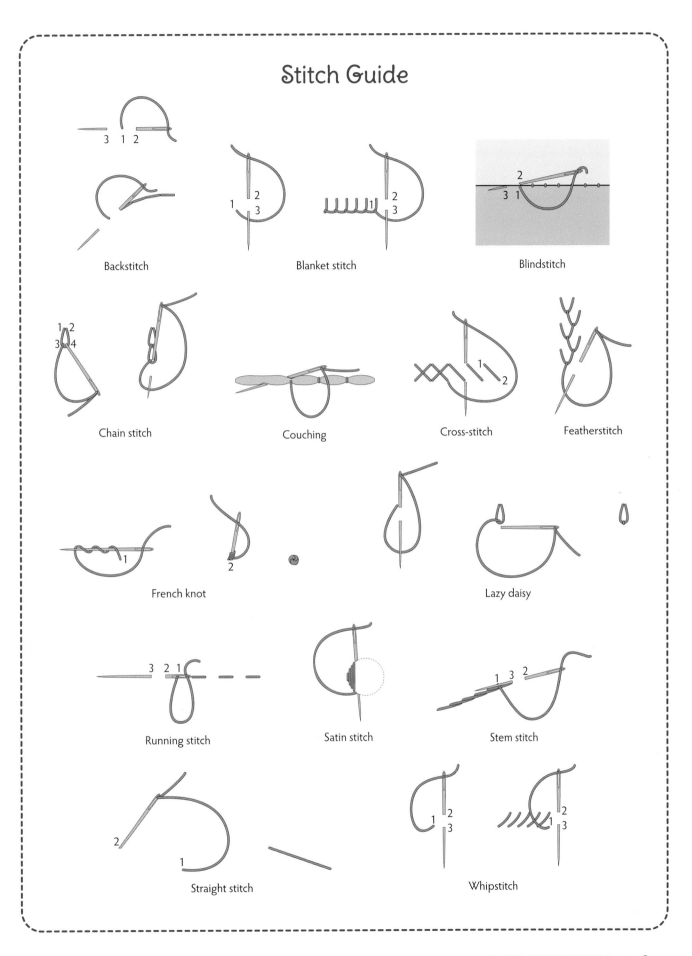

Backstitch

Blanket stitch

Blindstitch

Chain stitch

Couching

Cross-stitch

Featherstitch

French knot

Lazy daisy

Running stitch

Satin stitch

Stem stitch

Straight stitch

Whipstitch

Cookie Cutouts

Get a jump on your holiday preparations by "baking" these calorie-free sweet treats any month of the year. Don't worry—this is one batch of cookies that will keep!

Gingerbread Duo Ornaments

FINISHED SIZE: 4¼" × 5½"

Materials for Both Ornaments

- 6" × 9" piece of brown wool for bodies
- 3" × 4" piece of brown plaid wool for skirt
- 1" × 3" piece of green wool for bow tie
- 2" × 2" square of red wool for bow and heart
- 4 pieces, 5½" × 7", of black wool for gingerbread body outlines and backs
- 4 black buttons for eyes, ⅛" diameter
- 3 black buttons for tummy, ³⁄₁₆" diameter
- Size 12 pearl cotton in brown, cream, green, and red
- Black sewing thread
- Embroidery and hand-sewing needles
- 16" of thin twine for hangers

Stitching and Assembly

1. Use the patterns (page 16) to cut two small gingerbread bodies and the skirt, bow tie, hair bow, and heart from the wool as directed.

2. Position and pin a gingerbread body and the green bow tie on one black wool 5½" × 7" piece. Blanket-stitch with coordinating pearl cotton. Using brown pearl cotton, backstitch around the body close to the ends of the blanket stitching.

3 Using green pearl cotton, sew straight stitches to outline the bow tie. Using red pearl cotton, make three French knots for berries in the center of the bow tie. Using cream pearl cotton, sew a chain stitch across the head, arms, and legs in a zigzag formation.

4 Position and pin the remaining gingerbread body and skirt on a second black wool 5½" × 7" piece. Blanket-stitch with brown pearl cotton. Backstitch around the skirt close to the ends of the blanket stitching.

5 Position the bow and heart on the gingerbread body from step 4 and whipstitch in place with red pearl cotton.

6 Using cream pearl cotton, sew a chain stitch across the head, arms, legs, and across the bottom of the skirt in a zigzag formation. Using red pearl cotton, sew straight stitches to outline the bow and make a few straight stitches across the center of the bow from top to bottom. Make five French knots across the skirt just above the chain stitches. Using green pearl cotton, sew a lazy daisy stitch to the right of each French knot and sew two lazy daisy stitches at the top center of the heart.

7 Sew the buttons in place for the eyes on each ornament. Sew the three black buttons in place on the bow-tie ornament.

8 Using black thread, sew the mouths, eyebrows, and lashes onto the gingerbread ornaments using a backstitch.

9 Cut away the excess black wool ¼" from the edge of the gingerbread bodies. Position and pin a front onto a black wool 5½" × 7" piece. Trim the black wool even with the edges of the front. Using black pearl cotton, blanket-stitch around the edges, joining the front and back.

10 Press. Cut the twine in half to make two 8" lengths. Thread a length of twine through the top of each ornament for hanging.

Bow Tie Gingerbread Ornament

FINISHED SIZE: 5½" × 7"

Materials

- ✗ 6" × 7½" piece of brown wool for body
- ✗ 2 pieces, 7" × 8", of black wool for front and back
- ✗ 2 white buttons for tummy, ¾" and 1" diameter
- ✗ 2 black buttons for eyes, ³⁄₁₆" diameter
- ✗ 12" piece of ½"-wide white ribbon for bow
- ✗ 8" length of cord or yarn for hanger
- ✗ Size 12 pearl cotton in black, brown, and cream
- ✗ Embroidery and hand-sewing needles

Stitching and Assembly

1 Use the pattern (page 16) to cut a large gingerbread body from brown wool.

2 Position and pin the gingerbread body onto a black wool 7" × 8" piece. Blanket-stitch with brown pearl cotton.

Raid Your Mom's Button Box

Part of the charm of this guy is the mismatched buttons and vintage-looking bow. Check your mom's button box for just the right embellishments.

3 Using cream pearl cotton, sew around the inside of the blanket stitching using a featherstitch.

4 Sew the black buttons in place for the eyes and sew the white buttons in place on the tummy.

5 Tie the ribbon in a bow and tack it in place at the neck.

6 Cut away the excess black wool ¼" from the edge of the gingerbread body. Position and pin the front onto the remaining black wool piece. Trim the black wool piece even with the edges of the front. Using black pearl cotton, blanket-stitch around the edges, joining the front and back pieces.

7 Thread the cord through the top of the ornament for hanging.

Holly Necklace Bowl Filler
FINISHED SIZE: 5½" × 7"

Materials

- 6" × 7½" piece of brown plaid wool for gingerbread body
- 7" × 8" piece of black wool for gingerbread body outline
- 8" × 9" piece of brown check cotton for front
- 8" × 9" piece of tan check cotton for back
- 1" × 3" piece of brown plaid wool for closure covering
- 26" length of cream wool yarn
- 4 white buttons for tummy, ½" diameter
- 2 black buttons for eyes, ⅛" diameter
- Size 12 pearl cotton in black, brown, green, and red
- Embroidery and hand-sewing needles
- Fiberfill stuffing

Stitching and Assembly

1 Use the pattern (page 16) to cut a large gingerbread body from brown plaid wool.

2 Position and pin the gingerbread body on the black wool 7" × 8" piece. Blanket-stitch with brown pearl cotton.

3 Using coordinating sewing thread, couch over the cream wool yarn in a line around the inside of the blanket stitching.

4 Sew the buttons in place for the eyes.

5 Using red pearl cotton, sew circles for cheeks using a backstitch and fill in the center of the circles with a satin stitch.

6 Using a double strand of green pearl cotton, sew a chain stitch across the neck of the body. Sew random lazy daisy stitches for leaves on each side of the chain stitches. Using a double strand of red pearl cotton, make several French knots across the neck for berries.

7 Cut away the excess black wool ¼" from the edge of the gingerbread body. Position and pin the front onto the brown check cotton 8" × 9" piece. Using black pearl cotton, blanket-stitch the outlined gingerbread body to the brown check. Press.

Customized Cookies

Decorating your gingerbread ornaments and bowl fillers can be just as fun as decorating cutout cookies. They don't all have to look the same. Decorate each to suit your personality!

8 Place the tan check 8" × 9" piece right side up on your work surface. Place the embroidered gingerbread design, right side down, on the top. Pin all layers together and press flat. Using the outer edge of the blanket stitching of the black wool outline as a guide, machine sew ¼" from the edge of the black outline; do not leave an opening.

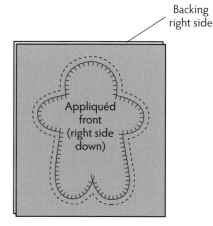

Sew ¼" from black wool outline.

9 Trim away all excess fabric, leaving a ¼" seam allowance; clip corners.

10 Referring to "Assembling Bowl Fillers and Small Pillows" (page 27), cut a slit in the back, turn right side out, and stuff the bowl filler. Cover the closed opening with the 1" × 3" piece of brown plaid wool and whipstitch around the edges using matching pearl cotton.

11 Sew two white buttons in place on the gingerbread cookie tummy using a long needle and sewing from front to back, placing the other two white buttons on the back of the gingerbread body and pulling your thread taut as you sew the buttons on.

Heart Patch Bowl Filler

FINISHED SIZE: 5½" × 7"

Materials

- Brown wool:
  - 6½" × 7½" piece for gingerbread body
  - 8" × 9" piece for back
- 7" × 8" piece of black wool for gingerbread body outline
- 2" × 2" square of light red wool for large heart
- 1" × 1½" piece of dark red wool for small heart
- 8" × 9" piece of brown stripe cotton for front
- 1" × 3" piece of brown plaid wool for closure covering
- 26" length of ¾6"-wide cream rickrack
- 2 black buttons for tummy, ⅝6" diameter
- 2 black buttons for eyes, ⅜6" diameter
- Size 12 pearl cotton in black, brown, and red
- Sewing thread or embroidery floss in cream and red
- Embroidery and hand-sewing needles
- Fiberfill stuffing

Stitching and Assembly

1 Use the patterns (pages 16–17) to cut one large gingerbread body and the large and small hearts from the wool as directed.

2 Position and pin the gingerbread body on the black wool 7" × 8" piece. Blanket-stitch with brown pearl cotton.

3 Using one strand of tan sewing thread, couch over the rickrack in a line around the inside of the blanket stitching.

4 Position and pin the hearts to the gingerbread body. Whipstitch with red pearl cotton. Using black pearl cotton, sew long straight stitches randomly around the large heart, making a few of them cross-stitches.

5 Sew the smaller buttons in place for the eyes and the larger ones on the tummy.

6 Using a single strand of red sewing thread, sew straight stitches for cheeks, making three rows horizontally and two rows vertically.

7 Cut away the excess black wool to ¼" from the edge of the gingerbread body. Position and pin the front onto the brown stripe cotton 8" × 9" piece. Using black pearl cotton, blanket-stitch the gingerbread body to the brown stripe. Press.

8 Complete the bowl filler referring to steps 8–10 of assembling the Holly Necklace Bowl Filler (page 14).

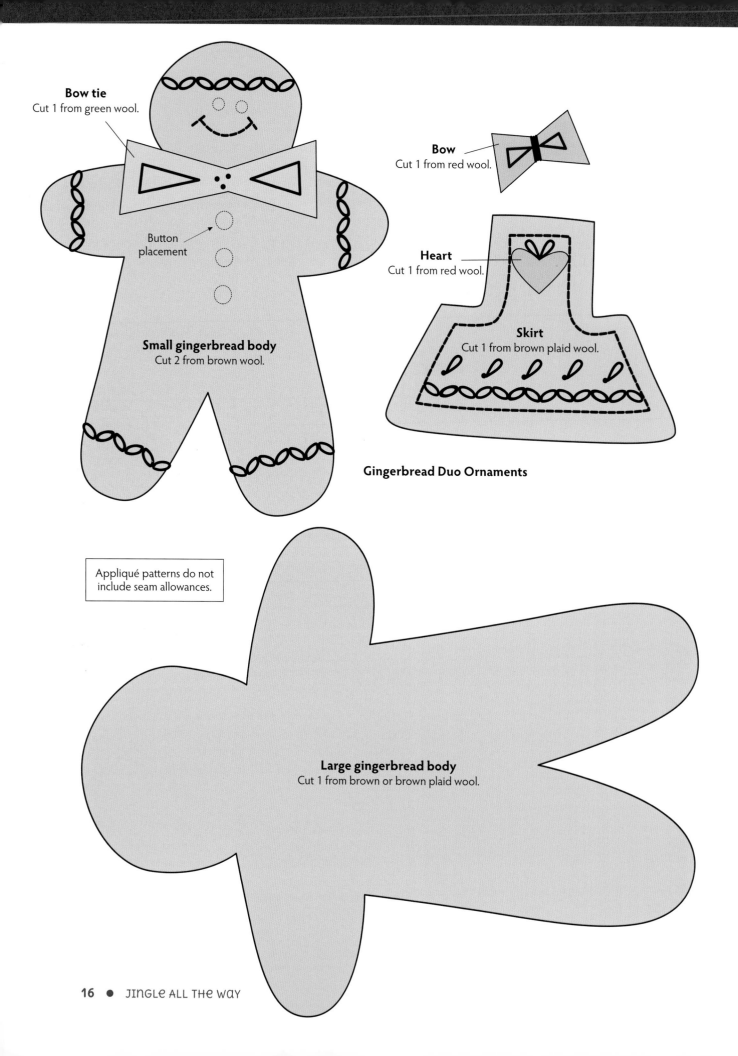

Bow tie
Cut 1 from green wool.

Button placement

Small gingerbread body
Cut 2 from brown wool.

Bow
Cut 1 from red wool.

Heart
Cut 1 from red wool.

Skirt
Cut 1 from brown plaid wool.

Gingerbread Duo Ornaments

Appliqué patterns do not include seam allowances.

Large gingerbread body
Cut 1 from brown or brown plaid wool.

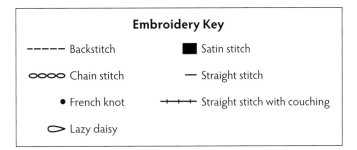

Embroidery Key

- - - - - Backstitch ▪ Satin stitch

ᴼᴼᴼᴼᴼ Chain stitch — Straight stitch

● French knot ++++ Straight stitch with couching

⌒ Lazy daisy

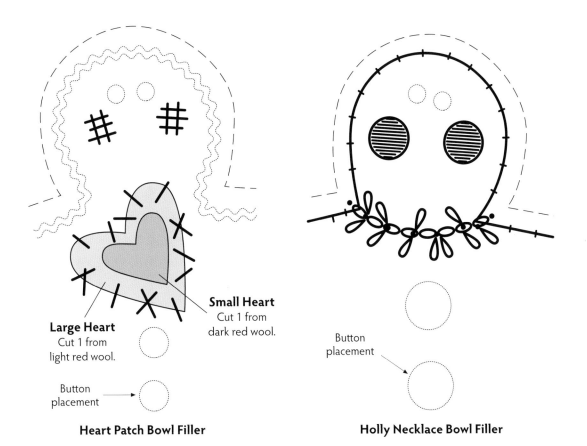

Large Heart
Cut 1 from
light red wool.

Small Heart
Cut 1 from
dark red wool.

Button
placement

Heart Patch Bowl Filler

Button
placement

Holly Necklace Bowl Filler

Season's Greetings

Proclaim your love of the season with an itty-bitty windowpane quilt and coordinating bowl fillers. Wool appliqué and simple embroidery stitches make all of these fun to stitch, and they're perfect for gift giving too.

Merry Wishes Mini Quilt

FINISHED QUILT: 10½" × 16¼"
FINISHED BLOCKS: 3½" × 3¾"

Materials

Yardage is based on 42"-wide fabric.

- ¼ yard of dark gray solid cotton for block backgrounds
- 3" × 3½" piece of green stripe wool for stocking in Stocking block
- 4" × 7" piece of red wool for heel, toe, and heart in Stocking block; candy cane in Candy Cane block; letters J and Y in Joy block; and berry in Gift block
- 2" × 2½" piece of cream wool for cuff in Stocking block and bow in Bell block
- 2½" × 6½" piece of light green wool for bow in Candy Cane block, wreath in Joy block, tree in Tree block, and trim in Bell block
- 1½" × 2½" piece of dark green wool for holly leaves in Gift block
- 3" × 3" square of green plaid wool for present in Gift block
- 3" × 6" piece of red plaid wool for ribbon and lid in Gift block, trim in Tree block, and bell in Bell block
- 1" × 2" piece of gold wool for star in Tree block and striker in Bell block
- 1½" × 1½" square of brown wool for trunk in Tree block
- ¼ yard of black-and-white stripe cotton for sashing and border

Continued on page 20

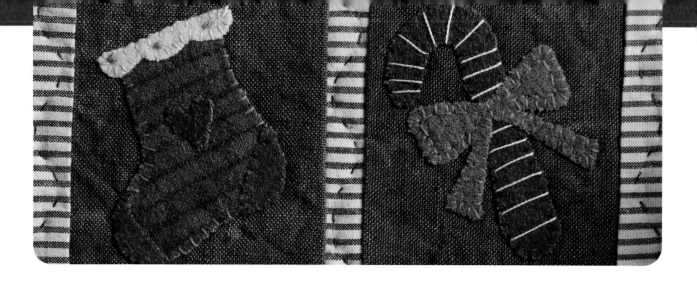

Continued from page 19

- ✕ ½ yard of black stripe cotton for backing and self-binding
- ✕ 14" × 20" piece of batting
- ✕ Size 12 pearl cotton in black, brown, cream, gray, green, red, and variegated gold
- ✕ Embroidery and hand-sewing needles

Cutting

All measurements include ¼"-wide seam allowances.

From the dark gray solid, cut:
1 strip, 5" × 42"; crosscut into 6 squares, 5" × 5"

From the black-and-white stripe, cut:
2 strips, 1¾" × 42"; crosscut into:
    2 strips, 1¾" × 16¼"
    2 strips, 1¾" × 8"
1 strip, 1½" × 42"; crosscut into 2 strips, 1½" × 8"
1 strip, 1" × 42"; crosscut into 3 pieces, 1" × 4¼"

Assembling the Quilt

Press the seam allowances as shown by the arrows.

1 Use the patterns (pages 21-22) to cut the appliqué pieces for the six blocks from the wool as directed.

2 Position and pin the pieces for each block onto a dark gray 5" square. Whipstitch all the pieces in place with coordinating pearl cotton. Embroider using pearl cotton and the embroidery key for each block.

3 Centering the design, trim each block to 4" wide × 4¼" tall, including seam allowances.

4 Referring to the quilt assembly diagram, sew together the blocks and black-and-white 1" × 4¼" pieces in three horizontal rows. Join the rows with the black-and-white 1½" × 8" strips to make the quilt center, which should be 8" × 13¾", including seam allowances. Sew the black-and-white 1¾" × 8" border strips to the top and bottom of the quilt center and the 1¾" × 16¼" border strips to the sides to complete the quilt top, which should be 10½" × 16¼".

Quilt assembly

5 Place the black stripe fabric wrong side up on your work surface and center the batting 14" × 20" piece on top. Center the quilt top right side up on top and baste the layers together. Using black pearl cotton and a running stitch, stitch through the sashing to quilt the mini quilt. Carefully trim the batting even with the quilt top.

6 Trim the excess backing, leaving 1" beyond the quilt top, which will be used to bind the quilt.

Trim backing.

7 To miter each corner, trim the backing at a 45° angle, ½" from each corner of the quilt top. Fold the trimmed edge in ½". Fold under the adjacent edges ½" twice; hand stitch this binding in place on the quilt top.

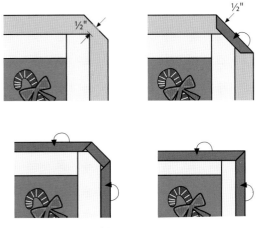

Miter corners.

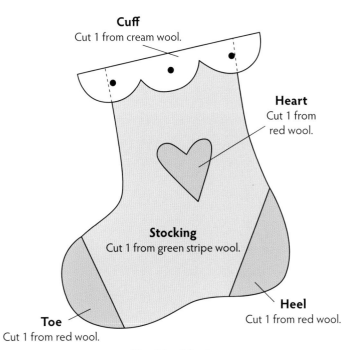

Cuff
Cut 1 from cream wool.

Heart
Cut 1 from red wool.

Stocking
Cut 1 from green stripe wool.

Heel
Cut 1 from red wool.

Toe
Cut 1 from red wool.

Stocking block

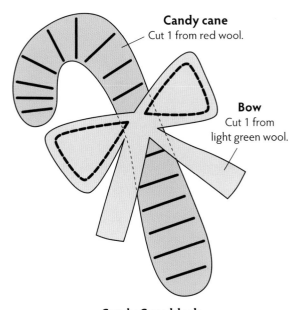

Candy cane
Cut 1 from red wool.

Bow
Cut 1 from light green wool.

Candy Cane block

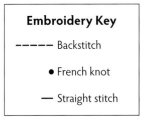

Embroidery Key

----- Backstitch

● French knot

— Straight stitch

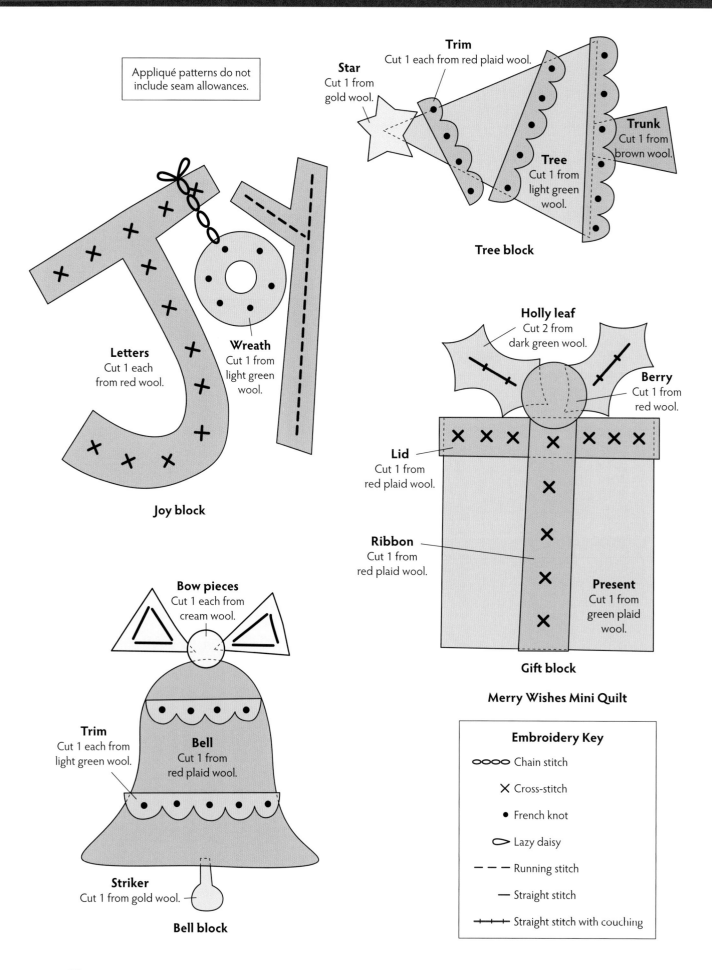

Appliqué patterns do not include seam allowances.

Star
Cut 1 from gold wool.

Trim
Cut 1 each from red plaid wool.

Trunk
Cut 1 from brown wool.

Tree
Cut 1 from light green wool.

Tree block

Letters
Cut 1 each from red wool.

Wreath
Cut 1 from light green wool.

Joy block

Holly leaf
Cut 2 from dark green wool.

Berry
Cut 1 from red wool.

Lid
Cut 1 from red plaid wool.

Ribbon
Cut 1 from red plaid wool.

Present
Cut 1 from green plaid wool.

Gift block

Merry Wishes Mini Quilt

Bow pieces
Cut 1 each from cream wool.

Trim
Cut 1 each from light green wool.

Bell
Cut 1 from red plaid wool.

Striker
Cut 1 from gold wool.

Bell block

Embroidery Key

⚬⚬⚬⚬ Chain stitch

✕ Cross-stitch

● French knot

⚬ Lazy daisy

– – – Running stitch

— Straight stitch

+++++ Straight stitch with couching

Be Merry Bowl Filler

FINISHED SIZE: 5" × 5"

Materials

- ✕ 5½" × 5½" square of dark gray linen for front
- ✕ 5½" × 5½" square of red herringbone wool for back
- ✕ 4" × 4" square of red wool for letters
- ✕ 1" × 1½" piece of light green wool for holly leaves
- ✕ 1" × 2" piece of cream wool for berries
- ✕ 20" length of white chenille trim
- ✕ Size 12 pearl cotton in cream, green, and red
- ✕ Embroidery and hand-sewing needles
- ✕ Fiberfill stuffing

Stitching and Assembly

1 Use the patterns below to cut out the letter, holly leaf, and berry appliqués.

2 Position and pin the letters and holly leaves on the dark gray linen square. Whipstitch in place with coordinating pearl cotton.

3 Position the berries on the dark gray linen and secure each berry with a French knot in red pearl cotton. Using green pearl cotton, stitch a running stitch through the center of each letter.

4 Referring to "Assembling Bowl Fillers and Small Pillows" (page 27), sew and stuff the bowl filler.

5 Hand sew the chenille trim over the seam all the way around the bowl filler.

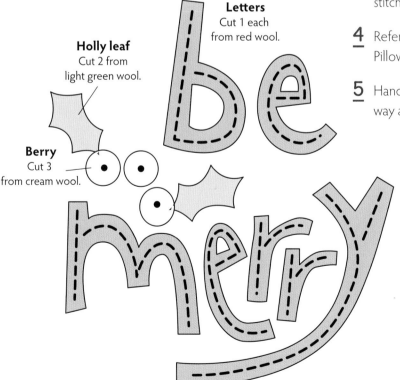

Holly leaf
Cut 2 from
light green wool.

Berry
Cut 3
from cream wool.

Letters
Cut 1 each
from red wool.

Be Merry Bowl Filler

Appliqué patterns do not
include seam allowances.

Embroidery Key
- ● French knot
- - - - - Running stitch

Joy Bowl Filler

FINISHED SIZE: 5" × 4½"

Materials

- ✕ 5" × 5½" piece of dark gray linen for front
- ✕ 5" × 5½" piece of dark red wool for back
- ✕ 4" × 4" square of red wool for letters *J* and *Y*
- ✕ 1½" × 1½" square of light green wool for wreath
- ✕ 19" length of white chenille trim
- ✕ Size 12 pearl cotton in cream, green, and red
- ✕ Embroidery and hand-sewing needles
- ✕ Fiberfill stuffing

Stitching and Assembly

1 Use the patterns below to cut out the letter and wreath appliqués.

2 Position and pin the letters and wreath on the dark gray linen piece. Blanket-stitch around the wreath with green pearl cotton. Whipstitch the letters with red pearl cotton.

3 Using red pearl cotton, make six French knots on the wreath. Using cream pearl cotton, sew long straight stitches across the letters. Using green pearl cotton, chain stitch from the top of the wreath to the top edge of the letter *J*. Make two lazy daisy stitches at the top of the chain stitching to make a bow.

4 Referring to "Assembling Bowl Fillers and Small Pillows" (page 27), sew and stuff the bowl filler.

5 Hand sew the chenille trim over the seam all the way around the bowl filler.

Appliqué patterns do not include seam allowances.

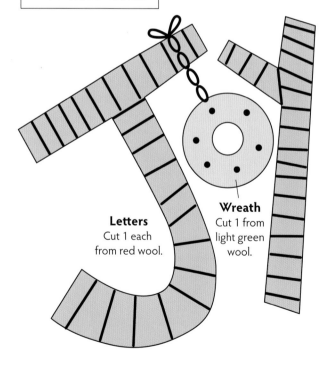

Letters
Cut 1 each from red wool.

Wreath
Cut 1 from light green wool.

Joy Bowl Filler

Embroidery Key

ᴏᴏᴏᴏ Chain stitch

• French knot

◠ Lazy daisy

— Straight stitch

Gift Bowl Filler
FINISHED SIZE: 4½" × 4½"

Materials

- × 5" × 5" square of dark gray linen for front
- × 5" × 5" square of gray wool for back
- × 3" × 3" square of red plaid wool for present
- × 2" × 3" piece of moss green wool for ribbon and lid
- × 1½" × 4" piece of green wool for holly leaves
- × 1" × 1" square of red wool for berry
- × 1" × 1½" piece of tan wool for tag
- × 18" length of white chenille trim
- × Size 12 pearl cotton in black, green, red, and tan
- × Embroidery and hand-sewing needles
- × Fiberfill stuffing

Stitching and Assembly

1 Use the patterns below to cut out the present, ribbon, lid, holly leaf, berry, and tag appliqués.

2 Position and pin the pieces on the dark gray linen square. Whipstitch each piece with coordinating pearl cotton.

3 Using tan pearl cotton, chain stitch from the top of the lid to the tag. Using black pearl cotton, backstitch the letters and add two French knots on the tag.

4 Referring to "Assembling Bowl Fillers and Small Pillows" (page 27), sew and stuff the bowl filler.

5 Hand sew the chenille trim over the seam all the way around the bowl filler.

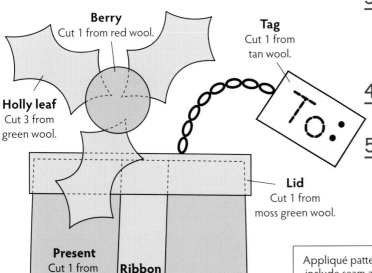

Berry
Cut 1 from red wool.

Tag
Cut 1 from tan wool.

Holly leaf
Cut 3 from green wool.

Lid
Cut 1 from moss green wool.

To:

Present
Cut 1 from red plaid wool.

Ribbon
Cut 1 from moss green wool.

Gift Bowl Filler

Appliqué patterns do not include seam allowances.

Embroidery Key

– – – – Backstitch

∞∞∞ Chain stitch

• French knot

Let It Snow Linen Bowl Filler
FINISHED SIZE: 6½" × 3½"

Materials

- × 4" × 7" piece of dark gray linen for front
- × 4" × 7" piece of gray wool for back
- × 1" × 3" piece of dark gray wool for opening cover
- × 20" length of white chenille trim
- × Size 12 pearl cotton in cream and gray
- × Embroidery and hand-sewing needles
- × Fiberfill stuffing

Stitching and Assembly

1 Transfer the words *Let it Snow* and the snowflakes from the pattern (page 27) onto the dark gray linen piece.

2 Backstitch the words using cream pearl cotton. Add a French knot to dot the *i*.

3 Embroider the snowflakes using cream pearl cotton with long straight stitches. Use a couching stitch over the center of the straight stitches to hold them in place. Embroider short straight stitches at the ends of the straight stitches in a V formation.

4 Referring to "Assembling Bowl Fillers and Small Pillows" (page 27), sew and stuff the pillow. Cover the closed opening with the piece of gray wool and whipstitch around the edges using gray pearl cotton. Optional: Using cream pearl cotton, make a snowflake on the gray wool piece on the back of the bowl filler.

5 Hand sew the chenille trim over the seam all the way around the bowl filler.

Let It Snow Linen Bowl Filler

Assembling Bowl Fillers and Small Pillows

When sewing together the front and back of pillows or bowl fillers (which are tiny pillows), there are two methods for creating an opening for stuffing.

Leaving an Opening

1 Place the front and back of the pillow right sides together, centering the front on the back. (The back will sometimes be larger than the front, but it will be trimmed even after stitching.) The pillow front should be wrong side up.

2 Using a ¼" seam allowance, sew around the edge of the pillow front and leave an opening along the bottom that's about 2" to 3" long.

3 Trim the excess fabric to make the seam allowances even. Trim the corners of the pieces. Clip the curves of round shapes.

4 Turn right side out through the opening and stuff lightly. Blindstitch the opening closed.

Cutting a Slit

1 Follow steps 1–3 of "Leaving an Opening," but sew all the way around; don't leave an opening.

2 Carefully cut an opening, about 1½" to 2" long, in the back of the pillow. *Be careful to cut only through the back layer.*

3 Turn the pillow right side out, stuff lightly, and whipstitch the opening closed. My favorite stuffing tool is a hemostat, which is helpful for grabbing and pushing small bits of stuffing into a pillow right where you need it. An alternative tool is a chopstick or knitting needle.

4 Cut a rectangular scrap of wool (or linen) large enough to cover the slit; whipstitch it over the top of the opening. For added fun, I sometimes embroider a word on the piece of wool before stitching it to the pillow back.

Happy Holly-Days

Set the stage—or your coffee table—with holiday spirit and this cute little wool mat. Carry the theme on to gift tags that replicate the look of a manila shipping label, complete with grommets for authenticity!

To You From Me Gift-Card Holder

FINISHED SIZE: 4½" × 6½"

Materials

Yardage is based on 42"-wide fabric.

- ✕ ¼ yard of black check cotton for front, back, and pocket
- ✕ 5" × 7" piece of cream wool for tag
- ✕ 3" × 3" square of green wool for holly leaves
- ✕ 1" × 4½" piece of red wool for ribbon band
- ✕ 16" length of white cord for hanger
- ✕ Size 12 pearl cotton in black, cream, green, and red
- ✕ 1 grommet, ½" diameter, and grommet tool
- ✕ 1 red button, ¾" diameter
- ✕ Embroidery needle

Cutting

All measurements include ¼"-wide seam allowances.

From the black check cotton, cut:
1 strip, 6" × 42"; crosscut into:
    1 piece, 6" × 10"
    2 pieces, 6" × 8"

Stitching and Assembly

1 Use the patterns (page 30) to cut out the tag, holly leaf, and ribbon band appliqués.

2 Position and pin the tag in the center of one black check 6" × 8" piece. Blanket-stitch around the tag using cream pearl cotton.

3 Transfer the words *To: You From: Me* onto the tag. Backstitch with black pearl cotton and make French knots for the dots. Press.

4 Position and pin the ribbon and leaves in place on the tag. Blanket-stitch using coordinating pearl cotton. Mark the circle for the hanger onto the tag and blanket-stitch around the circle. Press.

5 Sew the red button in place.

6 Place the remaining black check 6" × 8" piece right side up on your work surface. Fold the black check 6" × 10" piece in half widthwise with wrong sides together to make a 6" × 5" pocket; place the pocket on the first rectangle with the bottom raw edges aligned. Place the embroidered tag, wool side down, on the top. Pin all layers together and press flat. Using the outer edge of the blanket stitching of the tag as

a guide, machine sew ¼" from the edge of the tag, leaving a 2" opening.

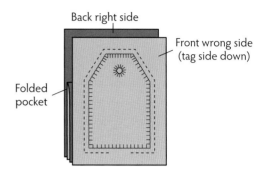

Back right side
Front wrong side (tag side down)
Folded pocket

7 Trim away all excess fabric, leaving ¼" seam allowances; clip corners. Turn right side out and press. Blindstitch the bottom opening closed.

8 Following the manufacturer's instructions, insert a grommet into the marked circle for hanging. Fold the cord in half and tie a knot at the end. Insert it through the grommet and secure with a lark's head knot (see page 62).

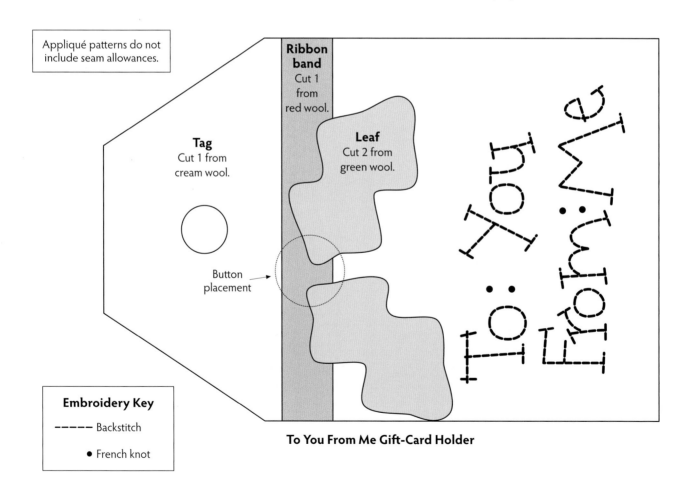

Appliqué patterns do not include seam allowances.

Ribbon band
Cut 1 from red wool.

Tag
Cut 1 from cream wool.

Leaf
Cut 2 from green wool.

Button placement

Embroidery Key

----- Backstitch

● French knot

To You From Me Gift-Card Holder

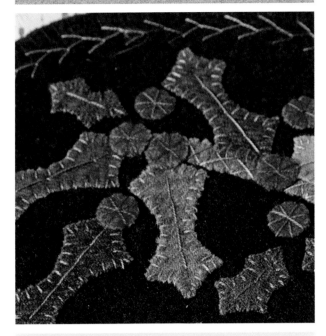

Oval Holly Christmas Mat

FINISHED SIZE: 13" × 9½"

Materials

- × 10½" × 29" piece of black wool for oval front and back
- × 3" × 9" piece of brown wool for branch
- × 3" × 3" square *each of 3* different green wools for large holly leaves
- × 3" × 7" piece of green plaid wool for small holly leaves
- × 3" × 4" piece of red wool for berries
- × Size 12 pearl cotton in black, brown, green, red, and tan
- × Embroidery needle

Stitching and Assembly

1 Use the patterns (page 32-33) to cut out two black background ovals and the branch, leaf, and berry appliqués as directed.

2 Referring to the photo on page 28, position and pin the branch and leaves onto a black oval. Whipstitch using brown pearl cotton. Then sew cross-stitches along the length of the branch.

3 Position and pin the leaves to the black oval. Whipstitch using green pearl cotton. Using tan pearl cotton, sew a long straight stitch along the center of each holly leaf and use a couching stitch over it to hold it in place.

4 Position and pin the red berries in place around the mat. Using red pearl cotton, use four straight stitches over each berry to make a star stitch. Make a small couching stitch across the center to hold the stitches in place.

5 Transfer the words *Merry Christmas* from the pattern onto the mat. Backstitch with tan pearl cotton.

6 Using red pearl cotton, sew a featherstitch around the border of the black oval. Press.

7 Center and pin the embroidered black wool oval onto the remaining oval. Blanket-stitch around the edges with black pearl cotton.

Appliqué and embroidery placement guide

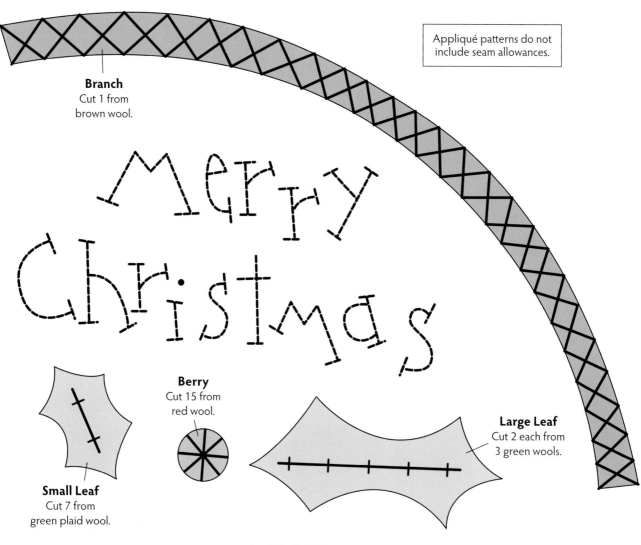

Appliqué patterns do not include seam allowances.

Branch
Cut 1 from brown wool.

Berry
Cut 15 from red wool.

Large Leaf
Cut 2 each from 3 green wools.

Small Leaf
Cut 7 from green plaid wool.

Oval Holly Christmas Mat

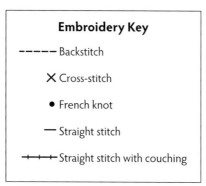

Embroidery Key

- - - - - Backstitch

✕ Cross-stitch

● French knot

— Straight stitch

++++ Straight stitch with couching

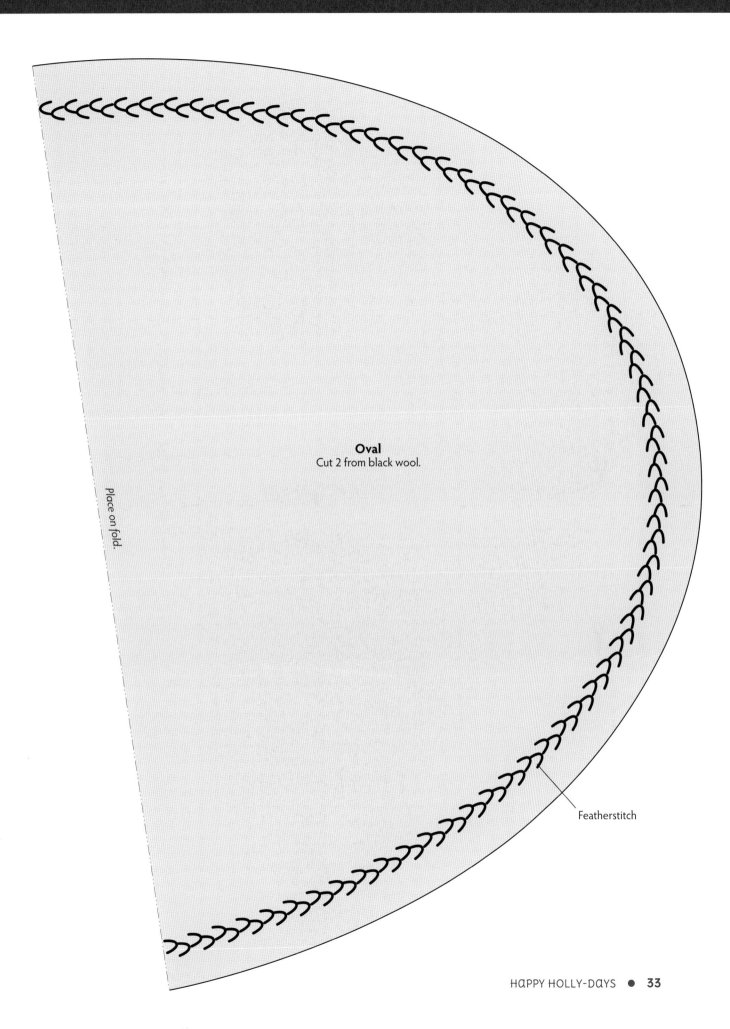

Oval
Cut 2 from black wool.

Place on fold.

Featherstitch

Letters to Santa

Don't expect to receive everything on your wish list if you don't mail your list to Santa! The post office may not accept your handmade postage stamps, but your family and friends surely will.

Express Mail Pillow

FINISHED SIZE: 9" × 6"

Materials

- ✕ 6½" × 9½" piece of tan linen for front
- ✕ 6½" × 9½" piece of green wool for back
- ✕ 7" × 7" square of red-and-cream stripe cotton for stripe appliqués
- ✕ 3" × 3" square of cream wool for stamp
- ✕ 2" × 2" square of green wool for stamp center
- ✕ 2" × 4" piece of gold wool for star
- ✕ Size 12 pearl cotton in black, cream, dark gray, gold, green, and red
- ✕ Gold quilting thread
- ✕ 1 red button for stamp, ½" diameter
- ✕ Embroidery and hand-sewing needle
- ✕ Fiberfill stuffing

Stitching and Assembly

1. Cut the red-and-cream stripe on the bias to make one strip, 1½" × 6½", and one strip, 1½" × 5½". Fold under one long edge of each strip ½" and press. Repeat to fold under and press the remaining long edge of each strip.

2. Use the patterns (page 44) to cut out the stamp, square, and star appliqués as directed.

3. Position and pin the prepared bias strips on the tan linen 6½" × 9½" piece. Blindstitch in place.

Two Layers for Stability

When using cotton as a background for wool appliqué, I often use two layers of background fabric. It adds stability to the project when stitching and creates a better layer when stuffing bowl fillers and pillows.

<u>4</u> Position and pin the stamp onto the tan linen piece. Whipstitch using cream pearl cotton.

<u>5</u> Position the green square in the center of the stamp. Blanket-stitch around the edges using green pearl cotton.

<u>6</u> Pin the two gold stars together and blanket-stitch around the edges using a single strand of gold quilting thread. Press and set aside.

<u>7</u> Transfer the words *express*, *To: Santa*, *north pole*, and *dec 25* and the remaining embroidery designs from the pattern onto the linen. Backstitch *Santa* using red pearl cotton. Backstitch *north pole* using green pearl cotton. Backstitch *To:* using black pearl cotton. Chain stitch the postage circle using gray pearl cotton. Backstitch the postage waves using black pearl cotton. Using
a single strand of gray sewing thread, backstitch *express*, the circle with *SC*, and *dec 25*. Press.

<u>8</u> Place the star in the center of the green square and secure with the red button on top.

<u>9</u> Referring to "Assembling Bowl Fillers and Small Pillows" (page 27), sew and stuff the pillow.

Christmas Star Stamp Ornament

FINISHED SIZE: 2¾" × 3¾"

Materials

- 2 pieces, 4" × 5", of black wool for stamp outline and back
- 3½" × 4½" piece of textured gray wool for stamp
- 2½" × 3" piece of cream wool for stamp center
- 2" × 2½" piece of gold wool for star
- 8" length of ⅛"-wide black ribbon for hanger
- Size 12 pearl cotton in black, brown, cream, gray, green, gold, and red
- Embroidery needle

Stitching and Assembly

1 Use the patterns (page 45) to cut out the stamp, rectangle, and star appliqués as directed.

2 Position and pin the stamp on one of the black wool pieces. Whipstitch with gray pearl cotton.

3 Position and pin the rectangle and star on the stamp. Blanket-stitch with coordinating pearl cotton. Press.

4 Using green pearl cotton, sew long straight stitches around the inside of the blanket stitching on the cream piece and make two cross-stitches on each side over the straight stitches.

5 Using brown pearl cotton, chain stitch from the top of the star to the top edge of the cream rectangle.

6 Using red pearl cotton, sew two lazy daisy stitches, a French knot, and two straight stitches to make a bow at the top of the star.

7 Cut away the excess black wool ⅛" from the edge of the stamp. Position and pin the front onto the remaining black wool piece. Trim the black wool piece even with the edges of the front. Using black pearl cotton, blanket-stitch around the edges, joining the front and back pieces.

8 Using the embroidery needle, poke each end of the black ribbon through to the front in the stamp top corners and tie in a knot for hanging.

Jingle Bell Stamp Ornament

FINISHED SIZE: 4¼" × 4¼"

Materials

- ✗ 2 squares, 5" × 5", of black wool for stamp outline and back
- ✗ 5" × 5" square of cream wool for stamp background
- ✗ 3" × 3" square of gray herringbone wool for bell
- ✗ ½" × 3" strip of dark gray wool for bell rim
- ✗ 1" × 1" square of dark green wool for small holly leaf
- ✗ 1" × 2" piece of green wool for large holly leaf
- ✗ 1" × 1" square of red wool for berry
- ✗ 8" length of ⅛"-wide black ribbon for hanger
- ✗ 12" length of ½"-wide sheer white ribbon for bow
- ✗ 3 silver bells, ¼" diameter
- ✗ Size 12 pearl cotton in black, cream, dark gray, green, light gray, and red
- ✗ Embroidery and hand-sewing needles

Stitching and Assembly

1 Use the patterns (page 45) to cut out the stamp, bell, bell rim, leaf, and berry appliqués as directed.

2 Position and pin the stamp and bell on a black wool 5" square. Blanket-stitch with coordinating pearl cotton. Using gray pearl cotton, chain stitch from the top of the bell to the top edge of the cream stamp.

3 Position and pin the dark green leaf and the bell rim on the bell. Whipstitch with coordinating pearl cotton. Press. Using light gray pearl cotton, make five French knots across the bell rim.

4 Position and pin the green leaf on the bell. Use green pearl cotton to sew a long straight stitch through the center of each leaf like a vein (the outer edges of the green leaf just added will not be stitched down).

5 Position the red berry and whipstitch using red pearl cotton.

6 Transfer the word *Jingle* from the pattern onto the top-right corner of the stamp and backstitch it using dark gray pearl cotton.

7 Cut away the excess black wool a scant ¼" from the edge of the stamp. Position and pin the front onto the remaining black wool 5" square. Trim the black wool piece even with the edges of the front. Using black pearl cotton, blanket-stitch around the edges, joining the front and back pieces.

8 Make a double bow using the sheer white ribbon and tack it at the top center of the cream stamp edge. Add three silver bells to the center of the bow.

9 Using the embroidery needle, poke each end of the black ribbon through to the back on the stamp upper edge and tie in a knot for hanging.

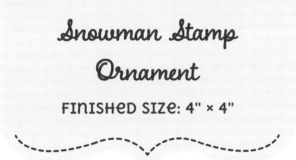

Snowman Stamp Ornament

FINISHED SIZE: 4" × 4"

Materials

- 2 squares, 5" × 5", of dark green wool for stamp outline and back
- 4½" × 4½" square of cream wool for stamp
- 3" × 3" square of tan wool for stamp-center background
- 2½" × 2½" square of cream wool for snowman
- 1" × 2" piece of black wool for hat
- 1½" × 2½" piece of dark green wool for scarf
- 1½" × 1½" square of green wool for holly leaf
- 1" × 1" square of red wool for berry
- Size 12 pearl cotton in black, cream, green, orange, red, and tan
- 22" length of ½"-wide red silk ribbon for hanger and bow
- 1 tan button, 1" diameter
- Embroidery and hand-sewing needles

Stitching and Assembly

1 Use the patterns (page 45) to cut out the stamp, square, snowman, hat, scarf, holly leaf, and berry appliqués as directed.

2 Position and pin the stamp and square appliqués on a dark green wool 5" square. Whipstitch the stamp with cream pearl cotton. Blanket-stitch around the square with tan pearl cotton and then backstitch around the inside of the blanket stitching on the square.

3 Position and pin the remaining appliqués in place on the tan square. Whipstitch with coordinating pearl cotton. Press.

4 Using black pearl cotton, make French knots for the snowman eyes, backstitch the mouth, and sew a long running stitch around the outside edge of the tan square.

5 Using orange pearl cotton, make two horizontal straight stitches for the snowman nose.

6 Using red pearl cotton, make three long straight stitches to make a hat brim.

7 Cut away the excess dark green wool ⅛" to ¼" from the edge of the stamp. Position and pin the front onto the remaining dark green wool 5" square. Trim the dark green wool piece even with the edges of the front. Using green pearl cotton, blanket-stitch around the edges, joining the front and back pieces.

8 Sew the tan button to the top of the stamp in the corner.

9 Cut the ribbon into a 10" length and a 12" length. Tie the 12" length around the button and then knot the ends to make a hanger. Tie the 10" length around the button and then tie in a bow. Trim the ends at an angle.

Gingerbread Stamp Ornament

FINISHED SIZE: 2¾" × 3¼"

Materials

- ✗ 2 pieces, 3½" × 4", of black wool for stamp outline and back
- ✗ 3½" × 4" piece of cream wool for stamp
- ✗ 2" × 2½" piece of brown wool for gingerbread body
- ✗ Size 12 pearl cotton in black, brown, cream, green, and red
- ✗ 6" length of ⅛"-wide black ribbon for hanger
- ✗ Embroidery needle

Stitching and Assembly

1 Use the patterns (page 46) to cut out the stamp and gingerbread appliqués as directed.

2 Position and pin the stamp and gingerbread onto one of the black wool pieces. Whipstitch with coordinating pearl cotton.

3 Using red pearl cotton, backstitch a rectangular shape on the inside edge of the stamp.

4 Using green pearl cotton, make three lazy daisy stitches on the gingerbread neck. Using red pearl cotton, make two French knots for berries.

5 Using black pearl cotton, make French knots for the eyes and tummy buttons.

6 Cut away the excess black wool ⅛" from the edge of the stamp. Position and pin the front onto the remaining black wool 3½" × 4" piece. Trim the black wool piece even with the edges of the front. Using black pearl cotton, blanket-stitch around the edges, joining the front and back pieces.

7 Using the embroidery needle, poke each end of the black ribbon through to the front in the stamp top corners and tie in knots for hanging.

The Elf Made Me Do It Ornament

FINISHED SIZE: 4¼" × 4¾"

Materials

- × 2 pieces, 5" × 5½", of black wool for stamp outline and back
- × 5" × 5½" piece of cream wool for stamp
- × 3" × 3¾" piece of green wool for stamp center
- × 2½" × 3½" piece of red wool for collar
- × 1" × 1" square of gold wool for buckle
- × 1" × 3½" strip of black wool for belt
- × 5 silver bells, ¼" diameter
- × 9" length of ¼"-wide black ribbon for hanger
- × Size 12 pearl cotton in black, cream, green, and red
- × Gold sewing thread
- × Embroidery and hand-sewing needles

Stitching and Assembly

1 Use the patterns (page 46) to cut out the stamp, stamp center, collar, belt, and buckle appliqués as directed.

2 Position and pin the stamp onto one of the black wool 5" × 5½" pieces. Whipstitch with cream pearl cotton.

3 Position and pin the stamp center and collar onto the stamp. Blanket-stitch around the stamp center and collar with coordinating pearl cotton.

4 Position the belt in place and whipstitch using black pearl cotton.

5 Position the buckle in place and whipstitch using a single strand of gold sewing thread. Press.

6 Transfer the words *the Elf Made Me do it* from the pattern onto the stamp center and backstitch using cream pearl cotton. Use a French knot to dot the letter *i*.

7 Cut away the excess black wool a scant ¼" from the edge of the stamp. Position and pin the front onto the remaining black wool 5" × 5½" piece. Trim the black wool piece even with the edges of the front. Using black pearl cotton, blanket-stitch around the edges, joining the front and back pieces.

8 Using the embroidery needle, poke each end of the black ribbon through to the front in the stamp top corners and tie in knots for hanging.

9 Sew a silver bell at the end of each collar point.

Do Not Open Ornament

FINISHED SIZE: 5" × 4¼"

Materials

- × 2 pieces, 5" × 5½", of dark green wool for stamp outline and back
- × 5" × 5½" piece of cream wool for stamp
- × 3" × 3" square of red wool for numbers
- × 14" length of ½"-wide red silk ribbon for hanger
- × Size 12 pearl cotton in black, cream, dark gray, green, and red
- × Embroidery needle

Stitching and Assembly

1 Use the patterns (page 46) to cut out the stamp and number appliqués as directed.

2 Position and pin the stamp onto one of the dark green wool pieces. Blanket-stitch around the stamp with cream pearl cotton.

3 Transfer the words *do not open til* and *dec.* from the pattern onto the stamp and backstitch them using dark gray pearl cotton. Use a French knot to dot the letter *i* and make a period after *dec.*

4 Position and pin the numbers in place on the stamp. Whipstitch with red pearl cotton.

5 Using black pearl cotton, sew straight stitches around the numbers to look like basting. Using green pearl cotton, sew French knots along the center of the red wool numbers.

6 Using a double strand of green pearl cotton and long straight stitches, make a rectangle centered on the stamp. Use a couching stitch to tack the straight stitches in place.

7 Using green pearl cotton, sew a lazy daisy stitch on each of the stamp's perforated points. Make a couching stitch on each side of the lazy daisy stitch to create the diamond shape.

8 Using red pearl cotton, make a French knot in the center of each lazy daisy stitch. Press.

9 Cut away the excess dark green wool a scant ¼" from the edge of the stamp. Position and pin the front onto the remaining dark green wool piece. Trim the dark green wool piece even with the edges of the front. Using green pearl cotton, blanket-stitch around the edges, joining the front and back pieces.

10 Thread the ends of the red ribbon from back to front at each corner and tie in knots for hanging.

Dear Santa, I Can Explain Ornament

FINISHED SIZE: 5¼" × 4½"

Materials

- 2 pieces, 5" × 6", of dark red wool for stamp outline and back
- 4½" × 5½" piece of cream wool for stamp
- 1½" × 4" strip of green wool for border
- 12" length of cream wool yarn for hanger
- 2 red buttons, ¾" diameter
- Size 12 pearl cotton in cream, green, and red
- Black sewing thread
- Embroidery and hand-sewing needles

Stitching and Assembly

1 Cut the green wool into two strips, ¼" × 3⅜", and two strips, ¼" × 3", for the border.

2 Use the pattern (page 44) to cut out the stamp from cream wool.

3 Position and pin the stamp onto one of the 5" × 6" pieces of dark red wool. Blanket-stitch around the edges using cream pearl cotton.

4 Position the green border strips on the stamp. Using green pearl cotton, sew cross-stitches over the strips to secure the border.

5 Transfer the words *dear Santa, i can explain…* onto the stamp and backstitch them using green pearl cotton. Use French knots to dot each letter *i* and make the ellipsis points.

6 Using a single strand of black sewing thread, make long straight stitches under each line of words; couch in place using tiny straight stitches. Press.

7 Cut away the excess dark red wool a scant ¼" from the edge of the stamp. Position and pin the front onto the remaining dark red wool piece. Trim the red wool piece even with the edges of the front. Using red pearl cotton, blanket-stitch around the edges, joining the front and back pieces.

8 Sew a red button to each upper corner.

9 Make a loop and tie a knot at each end of the wool yarn. Slip the loops over the buttons to make the hanger.

Stamp
Cut 1 from cream wool.

Border
Cut 1 from green wool.

Button placement

Appliqué patterns do not include seam allowances.

dear Santa,
i can
explain...

Embroidery Key

-------- Backstitch

∞∞∞ Chain stitch

✕ ✕ Cross-stitch

● French knot

+++ Straight stitch with couching

Dear Santa, I Can Explain Ornament

Button placement

express

dec 25

to: Santa
north pole

sc

Stamp
Cut 1 from cream wool.

Square
Cut 1 from green wool.

Star
Cut 2 from yellow wool.

Express Mail Pillow

Appliqué patterns do not include seam allowances.

Embroidery Key

- - - - - Backstitch
∞∞∞ Chain stitch
✕ ✕ Cross-stitch
● French knot
◯ Lazy daisy
– – – Running stitch
— Straight stitch

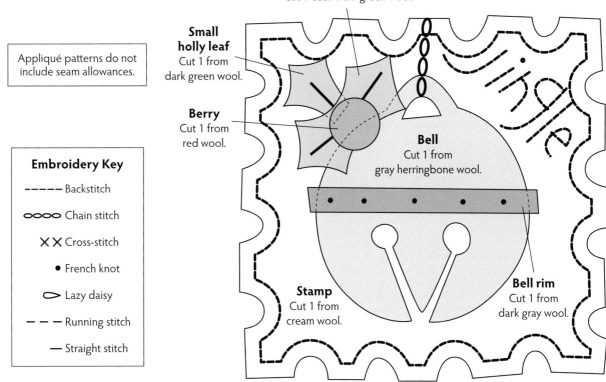

Large holly leaf
Cut 1 each from green wool.

Small holly leaf
Cut 1 from dark green wool.

Berry
Cut 1 from red wool.

Bell
Cut 1 from gray herringbone wool.

Stamp
Cut 1 from cream wool.

Bell rim
Cut 1 from dark gray wool.

Jingle Bell Stamp Ornament

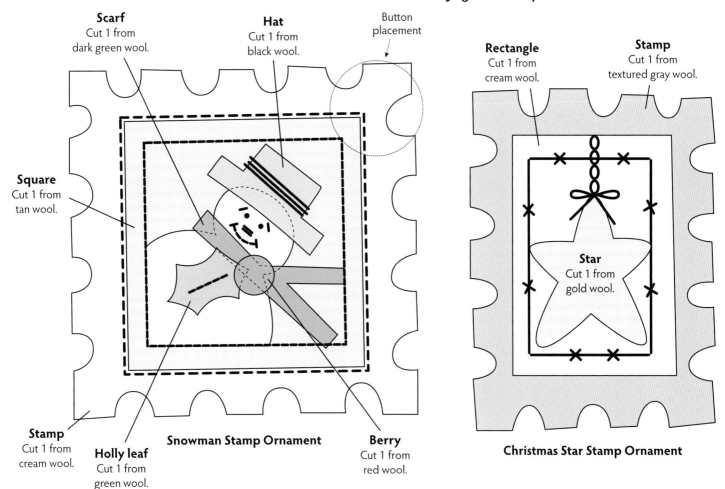

Scarf
Cut 1 from dark green wool.

Hat
Cut 1 from black wool.

Button placement

Square
Cut 1 from tan wool.

Stamp
Cut 1 from cream wool.

Holly leaf
Cut 1 from green wool.

Berry
Cut 1 from red wool.

Snowman Stamp Ornament

Rectangle
Cut 1 from cream wool.

Stamp
Cut 1 from textured gray wool.

Star
Cut 1 from gold wool.

Christmas Star Stamp Ornament

Belt
Cut 1 from black wool.

Buckle
Cut 1 from gold wool.

Stamp
Cut 1 from cream wool.

Collar
Cut 1 from red wool.

Stamp center
Cut 1 from green wool.

Bell placement

The Elf Made Me Do It Ornament

Appliqué patterns do not include seam allowances.

Embroidery Key

- - - - - Backstitch

• French knot

Lazy daisy

Lazy daisy with couching

— Straight stitch

+++++ Straight stitch with couching

Stamp
Cut 1 from cream wool.

Stamp
Cut 1 from cream wool.

Gingerbread
Cut 1 from brown wool.

do Not open til

dec.

Numbers
Cut 1 each from red wool.

Gingerbread Stamp Ornament

Poinsettia Wreath

Decorate your favorite seat in the house with a pretty three-dimensional poinsettia pillow. While I stitched my wreath to a pillow, you could use the same design as a table mat.

FINISHED SIZE: 20" × 20"

Materials

Yardage is based on 42" of usable fabric width.

- ¾ yard of moss green striped cotton for pillow front, border, and back
- 2 squares, 16" × 16", of thin cotton batting
- 10" × 18" piece of green wool for holly leaves
- 10" × 20" piece of dark red herringbone wool for medium poinsettia flowers
- 8" × 16" piece of dark red plaid wool for small poinsettia flowers
- 7" × 14" piece of red wool for extra-small poinsettia flowers
- ⅓ yard of red linen for large poinsettia flowers and extra-small poinsettia flowers
- Size 12 pearl cotton in gold, green, and red
- Red sewing thread
- 8 red buttons, ¾" diameter
- Fiberfill stuffing or 20"-square pillow form

Cutting

All measurements include ¼"-wide seam allowances.

From the *lengthwise grain* of the moss green stripe, cut:
2 strips, 2½" × 16½"

From the remainder of the moss green stripe, cut:
1 square, 20½" × 20½"
1 square, 16½" × 16½"
2 strips, 2½" × 20½"

Stitching and Assembly

Press the seam allowances as shown by the arrows.

1 Use the patterns (page 51) to cut out large leaves, medium poinsettias, small poinsettias, and extra-small poinsettias from wool as directed.

2 Place each pair of flower pieces wrong sides together. Blanket-stitch around the edges using coordinating pearl cotton. Press.

3 Using red pearl cotton, backstitch around the inside edge of the blanket stitching on each small flower.

4 Using red pearl cotton, sew a lazy daisy stitch on each petal of the extra-small flowers. Using gold pearl cotton, chain stitch a 1" diameter circle in the center of each flower. (Make sure to make the circle large enough so a ¾" button fits in the middle.) Press.

5 Fold the red linen ⅓-yard piece in half with right sides together to make a 12" × 20" piece. Using the large poinsettia and extra-small poinsettia patterns (page 51), trace around each flower four times. Machine stitch completely around on the traced lines. Trim away the excess fabric to a scant ¼" from each sewing line; clip the corners and curves. Cut a small slit through one layer only in the center of each flower. Turn right side out through the slit and press flat. Using red pearl cotton, blanket-stitch around the outside edge of the flower and featherstitch along the center of each flower petal.

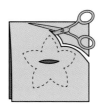

Stitch on drawn line, and trim.

6 Using gold pearl cotton, sew French knots in a 1"-diameter circle in the center of each extra-small linen flower. (Make sure to make the circle large enough so a ¾" button fits in the middle.)

7 Stack and layer the flowers in the following order: large linen flower, medium wool flower, small wool flower, and extra-small linen flower. As you layer them, rotate them so that all the petals show. Using red pearl cotton, sew through the center of all the flowers several times to secure. Using red pearl cotton, tack stitch at each inner junction of the flower to the flower below it so it stays secure and doesn't flop too much. Repeat to make four flower stacks.

8 Transfer the words *Merry Christmas* from the pattern (page 50) onto the center of the moss green stripe 16½" square, positioning the stripes horizontally. Backstitch using green pearl cotton. Make a French knot for the dot in the letter *i*.

9 Fold into quarters to mark center vertical and horizontal lines on the embroidered square to use as positioning lines.

10 Referring to the appliqué placement diagram, position the green wool leaves on the embroidered square, with one diagonally in each corner. Using green pearl cotton, blanket-stitch around the edges. Backstitch around the inside edge of the blanket stitching. Press.

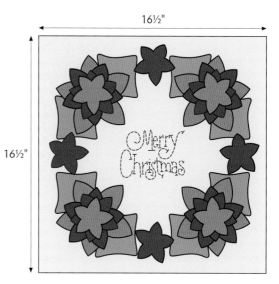

Appliqué placement

11 Layer the two batting 16" squares on the back of the embroidered and appliquéd square to provide support in the finished pillow.

12 Referring to the appliqué placement diagram (page 49), position a flower stack in the center of each leaf and sew in place with a button. Using a single strand of red sewing thread, blindstitch parts of the bottom flower petal to the pillow to keep them from flopping around on the finished pillow.

13 Position the four extra-small wool single flowers and attach them to the pillow by sewing a button in the center of each.

14 Sew the moss green stripe 2½" × 16½" strips to the side edges of the embroidered and appliquéd square. Add the moss green stripe

2½" × 20½" strips to the top and bottom edges to complete the pillow front.

Adding borders

15 Referring to "Assembling Bowl Fillers and Small Pillows" (page 27), use the appliquéd front and moss green stripe 20½" square to sew and stuff the pillow.

Poinsettia Wreath

Embroidery Key

- - - - Backstitch

● French knot

— Straight stitch

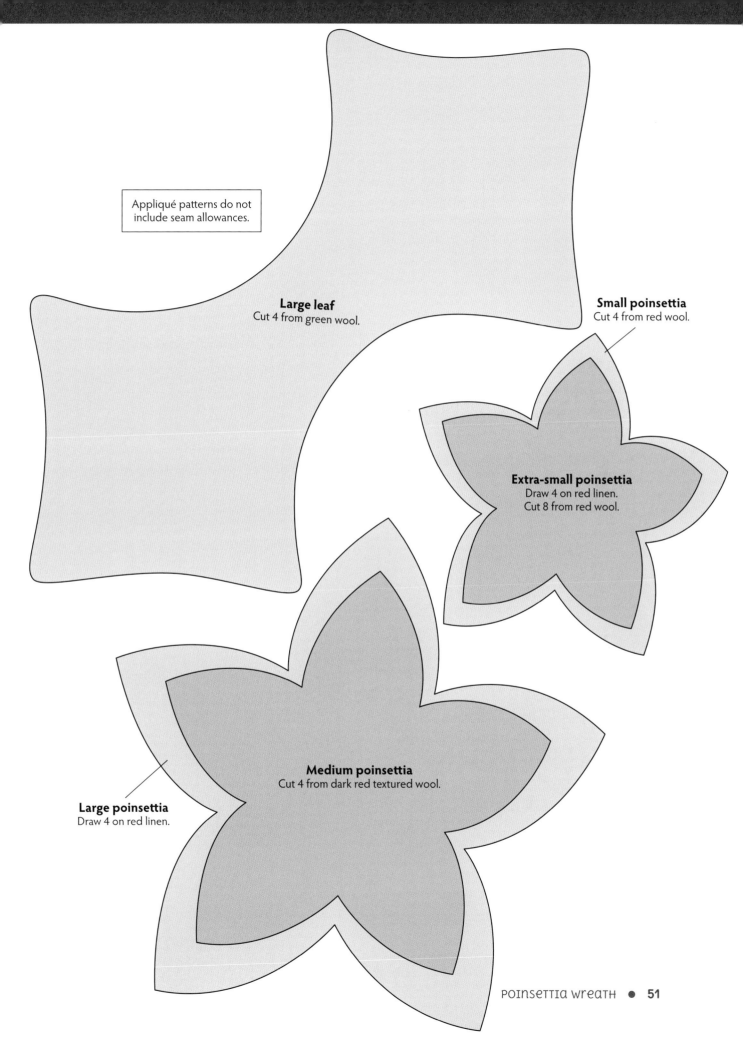

Appliqué patterns do not include seam allowances.

Large leaf
Cut 4 from green wool.

Small poinsettia
Cut 4 from red wool.

Extra-small poinsettia
Draw 4 on red linen.
Cut 8 from red wool.

Medium poinsettia
Cut 4 from dark red textured wool.

Large poinsettia
Draw 4 on red linen.

Sweet Petite Stocking

Whether you serve up a woolen stocking on a silver platter or you hang it on your front door, from the mantel, or tie it to a gift, one thing's for certain—you're going to want to make more than one!

FINISHED SIZE: 6½" × 9½"

Materials

- × 7½" × 20" piece of red plaid wool for stocking front and back
- × 6" × 6" square of white wool for cuff
- × 5" × 10" piece of green wool for toe, heel, and circles
- × 6 white buttons, ½" diameter
- × 45" length of white wool yarn for hanger
- × Size 12 pearl cotton in cream, green, red, and variegated green
- × Embroidery needle

Stitching and Assembly

1 Use the patterns (page 55) to cut out two stocking backgrounds and the cuff, toe, heel, and circle appliqués as directed.

2 Position and pin a toe and heel on each red plaid stocking background; be sure you turn one stocking over so you have two mirror-image pieces. Blanket-stitch the inner edge only of the toes and heels using variegated green pearl cotton. Backstitch along the inside edge of the blanket stitches.

3 Position and pin one cuff and three green circles on each red plaid stocking. Blanket-stitch around all edges using coordinating pearl cotton. Press.

4 Transfer the embroidery details on the cuff, toe, and heel from the pattern onto the stocking.

5 Using variegated green pearl cotton, sew a zigzag of straight stitches on the heel. At the point of each zigzag, make a French knot using cream pearl cotton.

6 Using variegated green pearl cotton, straight stitch five stems across the toe. Sew a long lazy daisy stitch on each side of the stems for leaves. Using red pearl cotton, make a French knot at the top of each stem.

7 Using green pearl cotton, sew a row of featherstitches across the top edge of the cuff. Using red pearl cotton, make a French knot at the end of each featherstitch.

8 Sew a button in the center of each green wool circle.

9 Pin the stocking front and back wrong sides together. Blanket-stitch around the outside edges with coordinating pearl cotton; leave the top edge open. Press.

10 Cut the wool yarn into three 15" lengths and braid them together, tying a knot at each end. Fold the braid in half and tack it to the edge of the cream cuff along the heel side of the stocking for the hanger.

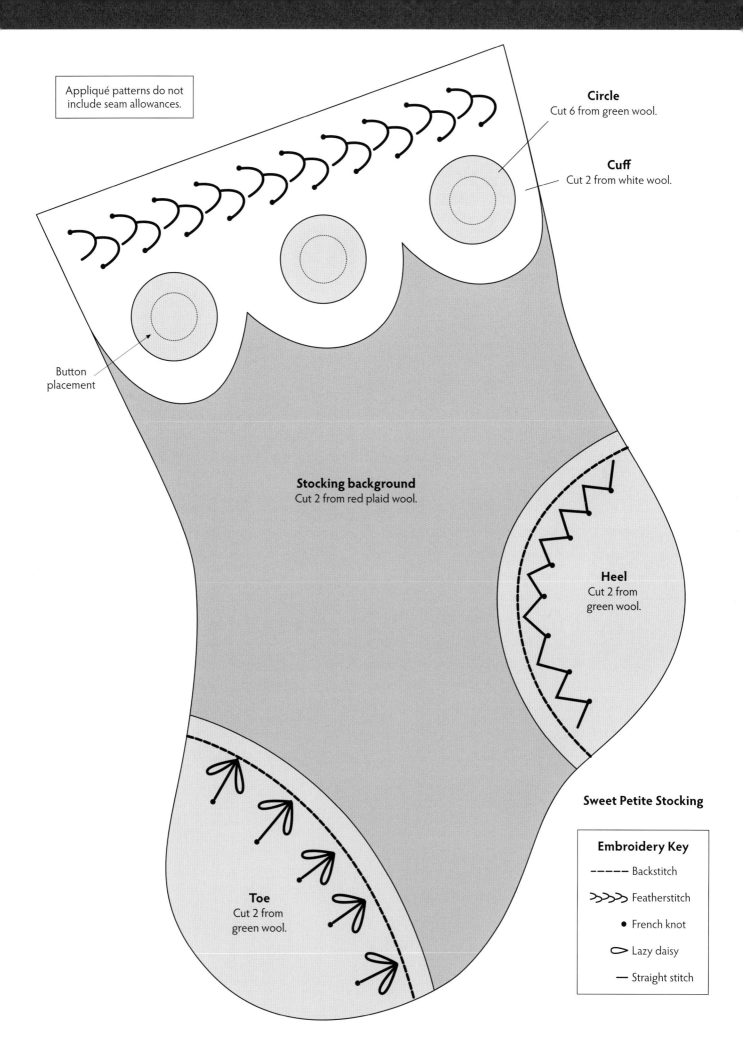

Appliqué patterns do not include seam allowances.

Circle
Cut 6 from green wool.

Cuff
Cut 2 from white wool.

Button placement

Stocking background
Cut 2 from red plaid wool.

Heel
Cut 2 from green wool.

Toe
Cut 2 from green wool.

Sweet Petite Stocking

Embroidery Key
- - - - - Backstitch

>>>> Featherstitch

• French knot

◯ Lazy daisy

— Straight stitch

Snow Flurries

Even if you live in a warm climate, you can make the snowflakes fly all winter long with this cute-as-a-button table mat. There's no need to pack it away until you're ready to celebrate spring.

FINISHED SIZE: 13" × 9½"

Materials

- ✕ 10½" × 14½" piece of black wool for front
- ✕ 10½" × 14½" piece of green wool for back
- ✕ 3" × 10" piece of brown wool for branch
- ✕ 3" × 4" piece of green wool for pine needles
- ✕ 6" × 8" piece of white wool for circles and snowflake
- ✕ Size 12 pearl cotton in black, brown, cream, and green
- ✕ Embroidery needle

Stitching and Assembly

1 Use the oval pattern from the Oval Holly Christmas Mat (page 33) to cut out one black and one green oval. Use the patterns (page 58) to cut the branch, pine needles, and snowflake appliqués as directed.

2 Position and pin the branch, snowflake, pine needles, and circles onto the black oval. Blanket-stitch around all pieces with coordinating pearl cotton.

3 Using brown pearl cotton, backstitch down the center of the branch.

4 Using cream pearl cotton, sew lazy daisy stitches at the ends of each snowflake point and each junction. Use a couching stitch to sew over the sides of the lazy daisy stitches to create a diamond instead of a loop. Make a French knot in the center of each lazy daisy stitch.

5 Transfer the snow flurry design from the pattern onto the mat. Using cream pearl cotton, backstitch the swirls and add French knots at the ends. Embroider each snowflake with short straight stitches. Press.

6 Center and pin the embroidered black wool oval onto the green wool oval, wrong sides together. Blanket-stitch around the edges with green pearl cotton. Sew a chain stitch around the inside edge of the blanket stitching using green pearl cotton. Press.

Appliqué patterns do not include seam allowances.

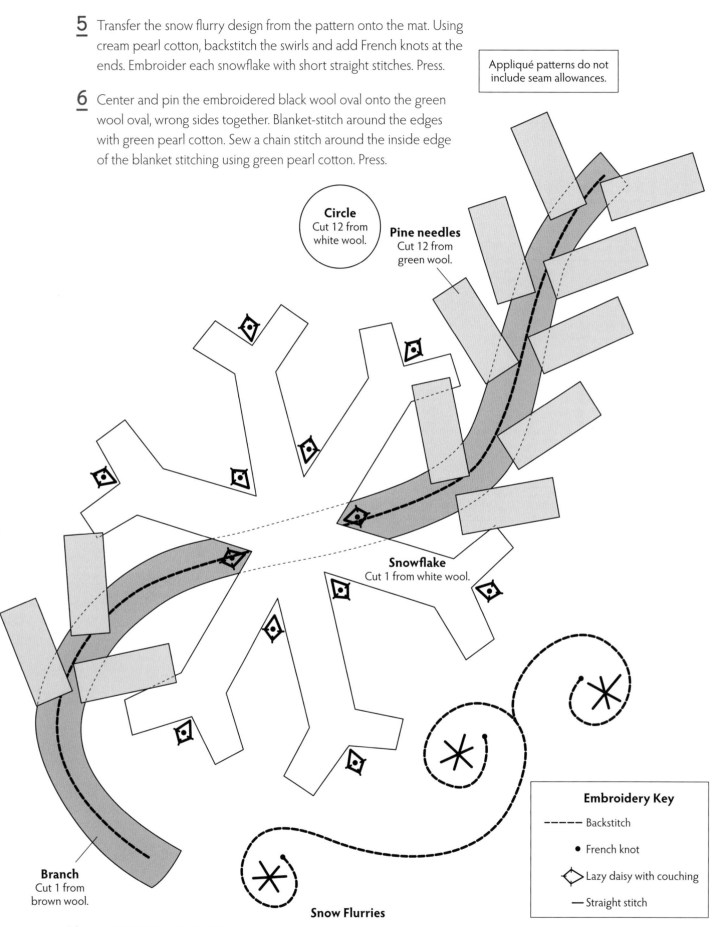

Circle
Cut 12 from white wool.

Pine needles
Cut 12 from green wool.

Snowflake
Cut 1 from white wool.

Branch
Cut 1 from brown wool.

Snow Flurries

Embroidery Key

------ Backstitch

• French knot

◇ Lazy daisy with couching

— Straight stitch

Dreaming of a White Christmas

Everyone can enjoy a white Christmas indoors, regardless of the weather outside. Stitch a little snowflake mat and set of ornaments to up the degree of festiveness in your home.

Round Snowflake Mat
FINISHED SIZE: 8" DIAMETER

Materials

- × 2 squares, 8" × 8", of black wool for front and back
- × 7" × 7" square of green wool for circle
- × 5" × 5" square of cream wool for snowflake
- × Size 12 pearl cotton in black, cream, and green

Stitching and Assembly

1 Use the patterns (page 63) to cut out two black background circles, the snowflake, and the circle appliqués as directed.

2 Position and pin the snowflake in the center of the green circle. Blanket-stitch around the edges using cream pearl cotton.

3 Transfer the border design from the pattern onto the green circle and backstitch with cream pearl cotton.

4 Using cream pearl cotton, embroider a snowflake in the center of the wool snowflake by crisscrossing long and short straight stitches over each other; tack the center with a couching stitch. Sew a French knot at the end of each long straight stitch. Sew little straight stitches in a V formation at the end of the short straight stitches.

Display Options

When embellished simply with embroidery, this mat will sit flat and is the perfect spot for a holiday candle. If you'd like to hang it as shown here, you may want to add button embellishments as I did on some of the ornaments.

5 Center and pin the green wool circle onto a black wool circle. Blanket-stitch around the edges with green pearl cotton.

6 Using green pearl cotton, featherstitch around the border of the black 8" circle. Using cream pearl cotton, make a French knot at the end of each featherstitch. Press.

7 Pin the remaining black wool circle to the wrong side of the embroidered circle. Blanket-stitch around the outside edges with black pearl cotton. Press.

Snowflake Ornaments

FINISHED SIZE: 5" × 5"

Materials for 1 Ornament

- ✕ 2 squares, 5½" × 5½", of black, red, or green wool for ornament front and back
- ✕ 5½" × 5½" square of cream wool for snowflake
- ✕ Size 12 pearl cotton in black, cream, green, and red
- ✕ 8" to 12" length of ½"-wide silk ribbon for hanger
- ✕ Optional: assorted cream buttons (the green ornament uses 12 buttons, ⅜" diameter, and 1 button, ⅞" diameter; the red ornament uses 6 buttons, ¼" diameter)

Stitching and Assembly

1 Use the pattern (page 63) to cut out a snowflake from cream wool.

2 Position and pin the snowflake onto a black, red, or green wool 5½" square. Blanket-stitch around all parts of the snowflake using cream pearl cotton. Press.

3 Referring to the photos at left and on page 61, add additional stitching (straight stitches, French knots) and buttons as desired.

4 Cut away the excess background wool a scant ¼" from the edge of the snowflake. Position and pin the front onto the remaining wool square. Trim the back wool square even with the edges of the front. Using coordinating pearl cotton, blanket-stitch around the edges, joining the front and back pieces.

5 Tie the ribbon ends together to make a hanger. Using the embroidery needle, poke a hole in one point of the snowflake and thread the ribbon loop through; tie the end in a lark's head knot (see below).

Lark's Head Knot

This type of knot is used in several projects in this book to make hangers. Fold a string or ribbon in half (tying the ends together if desired). Poke the loop at the fold through the top of the ornament, then pass the ends through the loop and tighten over the edge of the ornament.

Appliqué patterns do not include seam allowances.

Background circle
Cut 2 from
black wool.

Circle
Cut 1 from
green wool.

Snowflake
Cut 1 from
cream wool.

Round Snowflake Mat

Embroidery Key

- - - - - Backstitch

>>>>> Featherstitch

● French knot

— Straight stitch

Christmas Stitches

You're sure to spend many happy evenings embroidering these delightful motifs that you can enjoy for many Christmases to come. You could even make an extra set of blocks to use as stuffed bowl fillers or sachets!

FINISHED QUILT: 31½" × 39½"
FINISHED BLOCK: 6" × 6"

Materials

Yardage is based on 42"-wide fabric.

- ⅜ yard of taupe print for block backgrounds
- ⅓ yard of green plaid for block borders
- ¼ yard of light red stripe for sashing
- ⅝ yard of red solid for sashing and binding
- ¼ yard of light red check for sashing
- ⅜ yard of green solid for border
- 1¼ yards of fabric for backing
- 35" × 44" piece of batting
- Size 12 pearl cotton in black, brown, cream, gray, green, red, variegated gold, and variegated gray
- Embroidery needle

Cutting

All measurements include ¼"-wide seam allowances.

From the taupe print, cut:
2 strips, 5½" × 42"; crosscut into 12 squares, 5½" × 5½"

From the green plaid, cut:
7 strips, 1¼" × 42"; crosscut into:
    24 pieces, 1¼" × 6½"
    24 pieces, 1¼" × 5"

From the light red stripe, cut:
2 strips, 2½" × 42"; crosscut into 31 squares, 2½" × 2½"

From the red solid, cut:
8 strips, 2½" × 42"; crosscut *4 of the strips* into
    51 squares, 2½" × 2½"

From the light red check, cut:
2 strips, 2½" × 42"; crosscut into 31 squares, 2½" × 2½"

From the green solid, cut:
2 strips, 3" × 39½"
2 strips, 3" × 26½"

Assembling the Quilt Top

Press the seam allowances as shown by the arrows.

1 Transfer each of the 12 designs from the patterns (pages 67–69) onto the center of a taupe print 5½" square. Embroider using pearl cotton and the embroidery key for each block.

2 Centering the design, trim each embroidered taupe square to 5", including seam allowances.

3 Sew green plaid 1¼" × 5" strips to the top and bottom edges of a trimmed taupe square. Add green plaid 1¼" × 6½" strips to the sides to make a block. Make 12 blocks, each 6½" square, including seam allowances.

Make 12 blocks,
6½" × 6½".

4 Sew together one light red stripe, one red solid, and one light red check 2½" square in a row to make a sashing unit. Make 31 sashing units, each 2½" × 6½", including seam allowances.

Make 31 units,
2½" × 6½".

5 Lay out the remaining red 2½" squares, sashing units, and blocks in nine rows as shown in the quilt assembly diagram. Sew together the pieces in each row. Join the rows to make the quilt center, which should be 26½" × 34½", including seam allowances. Sew the green solid 3" × 26½" strips to the top and bottom edges of the

quilt center. Add the green solid 3" × 39½" strips to the sides to complete the quilt top, which should be 31½" × 39½".

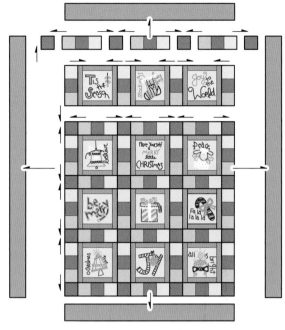

Quilt assembly

Finishing the Quilt

1 Prepare the quilt backing so it's about 4" larger in both directions than the quilt top.

2 Layer the quilt top with batting and backing; baste the layers together.

3 Quilt by hand or machine. My quilt is machine quilted with detail stitching around each embroidery, a wavy line in the block borders, arcs running from seam to seam in each square of the sashing, and holly leaves and spirals in the border.

4 Use the red solid 2½"-wide strips to make double-fold binding. Attach the binding to the quilt.

Embroidery Key

----- Backstitch   ◠ Lazy daisy

✕✕ Cross-stitch   ┼┼┼┼ Straight stitch with couching

• French knot

Season block

Stocking block

World block

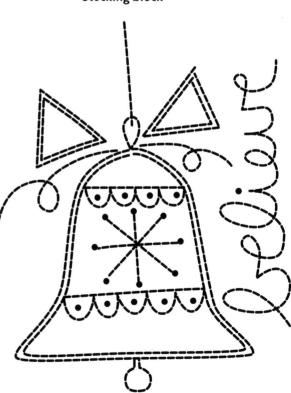

Bell block

Christmas Stitches

Have Yourself a MeRRY little CHRISTMAS

Little Christmas block

Peace block

Merry block

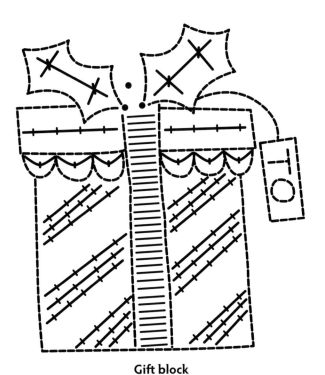

Gift block

Christmas Stitches

Embroidery Key

- - - - - Backstitch   ● French knot

oooo Chain stitch   ⬯ Lazy daisy

✕✕ Cross-stitch   — Straight stitch

Fa La La block

Tree block

Joy block

Christmas Stitches

Bright block

Sleigh Bells Sewing

What adorable gifts these pincushions and needle keeps will make for all your stitching friends. But don't forget to add yourself to the list as you'll surely want a set of these to keep!

Plum Pudding Pincushions

FINISHED SIZE: 3" × 3" × 2½"

Materials for 1 Pincushion

- ✕ 8" × 8" square of red check, green check, or red stripe cotton for pincushion
- ✕ 4" × 4" square of cream wool for frosting
- ✕ 3½" × 5" piece of green wool for holly leaves
- ✕ 1 bell, bead, or red wool ball for center detail (each ¼" to 1" diameter)
- ✕ 1 canning jar lid (the ones shown are vintage and are approximately 2½" diameter)
- ✕ Fiberfill stuffing
- ✕ Tacky glue
- ✕ Size 12 pearl cotton in cream, green, and red
- ✕ Embroidery needle
- ✕ Long needle and strong sewing thread

Stitching and Assembly

1 Use the patterns (page 76) to cut the frosting from cream wool and the circle from cotton. From the green wool, cut two using the large leaf pattern or use pinking shears to cut two using the small leaf pattern.

2 Position and pin the cream wool frosting appliqué in the center of the cotton fabric circle. Blanket-stitch around the edges using cream pearl cotton.

3 Backstitch or chain stitch around the inside edge of the blanket stitching using the color of your choice. Embroider the cream frosting as desired using one of the three pincushions shown as an example.

4 Sew a running stitch ¼" from the edge of the cotton fabric circle, leaving long thread tails.

5 Pull the long ends up to start gathering the circle and filling it with fiberfill stuffing. Stuff the pincushion as much as you can while pulling up the thread tails; tie a knot. If the pincushion isn't firm enough, add more fiberfill stuffing through the hole where the knot's tied using a hemostat or chopstick.

6 If you chose a large leaf: With wrong sides together, match the edges of the two large leaf green pieces. Blanket-stitch around the edges using green pearl cotton. Make a running stitch down the middle of the leaf, pulling it a bit to gather it. Tie the pearl cotton into a knot to hold the gathers.

7 Using a long needle and thread, sew through the center of the pincushion several times back and forth from top to bottom, pulling taut to create a dip in the center of the pincushion top.

8 Stitch the large or small leaf appliqué(s) and the chosen embellishment to the top center of the pincushion.

9 Spread glue around the inside of the jar lid on the bottom and all sides. Press the stuffed pincushion into the jar lid and hold in place for some time. *Do not remove* the pincushion once you've placed it in the glue.

Jingle Bell Needle Keeper

FINISHED SIZE: 4¼" × 4¾"

Materials

- × 10" × 10" square of gray herringbone wool for front and back
- × 4" × 4" square of black wool for background behind bell opening
- × 1" × 4½" strip of gray solid wool for bell rim
- × 3" × 3" square of green wool for leaves
- × 5" × 5" square of red solid wool for needle page
- × 5" × 5" square of green plaid wool for needle page
- × 1 red button for holly berry, ¾" diameter
- × Size 12 pearl cotton in gray, green, and red
- × 10" length of cream wool yarn for hanger

Stitching and Assembly

1 Use the patterns (page 77) to cut the needle-keeper body, circle, needle pages, bell rim, and leaves from the wool as directed. Only cut out the bell opening shapes on one of the bodies; this will be the needle-keeper front.

2 Center the black wool circle on the wrong side of the needle-keeper front. Using gray pearl cotton, blanket-stitch around the bell openings on the front.

3 Position and pin the gray solid bell rim to the needle-keeper front. Using gray pearl cotton, make cross-stitches over the bell rim to secure it in place. Using red pearl cotton, make a French knot in each space between the cross-stitches.

4 Place the needle-keeper front wrong sides together with a body piece, matching all edges. Using gray pearl cotton, blanket-stitch around the edges, joining the pieces. Backstitch just inside the inner edges of the blanket stitching. Using the two remaining needle-keeper body pieces, repeat to make the back.

5 Place the back on your work surface (wrong side up) and then layer the green plaid and red wool needle pages on top. Position the needle-keeper front, right side up, on top. Blanket-stitch through all layers around the top of the bell and inside the top bell opening.

6 Cross the two leaves over each other and sew to the top of the needle keeper with the button in the center.

7 Tie the cream wool yarn ends in a knot, then use a lark's head knot (see page 62) to tie the hanger to the top of the bell.

Jingle Bell Sewing Pocket Pouch

FINISHED SIZE: 4" × 5½" (CLOSED)

Materials

× 5½" × 14" piece of red plaid wool for outside

× 5½" × 14" piece of red check cotton for lining

× 3½" × 5" piece of textured green wool for large holly needle page

× 6" × 6" piece of dark green wool for pocket, small holly needle page, and small leaf appliqués

× 3" × 3" square of gray herringbone wool for bell appliqué

× 1" × 4" strip of red wool, cut with pinking shears, to cover strap

× 1 snap for closure, ½" diameter

× 3 red buttons: ½" diameter for holly berry, ¾" diameter for needle pages, and 1" diameter for flap

× Size 12 pearl cotton in cream, gray, green, and red

× 30" length of ⅛"-wide black cord for strap

× Embroidery needle

Stitching and Assembly

1 Use the patterns (page 78) to cut the pouch body, pocket, holly needle pages, bell, and small leaf appliqués from the wool and cotton as directed.

2 Referring to the appliqué placement diagram, position and pin the bell and small leaf appliqués on the red plaid pouch body. Blanket-stitch with coordinating pearl cotton.

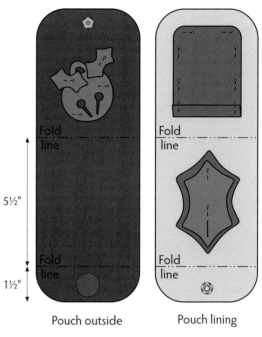

Pouch outside   Pouch lining

Appliqué placement

3 Using gray pearl cotton, chain stitch across the bell. Using cream pearl cotton, chain stitch from the top of the bell to the top of the pouch body. Sew the ½" button to the leaves for a berry.

4 Fold the top ½" of the pocket down to the right side and blanket-stitch in place using red pearl cotton. Referring to the appliqué placement diagram, position and pin the pocket on the red check cotton pouch lining. Blanket-stitch the curved side and lower edge with red pearl cotton, leaving the top edge open. Sew the ¾" button and the snap to the pouch as shown in the applique placement diagram above.

New Notions!

If you're making this pouch as a gift, tuck in a little something extra, such as a package of embroidery needles and a needle threader. While you're at it, treat yourself to a few new notions too!

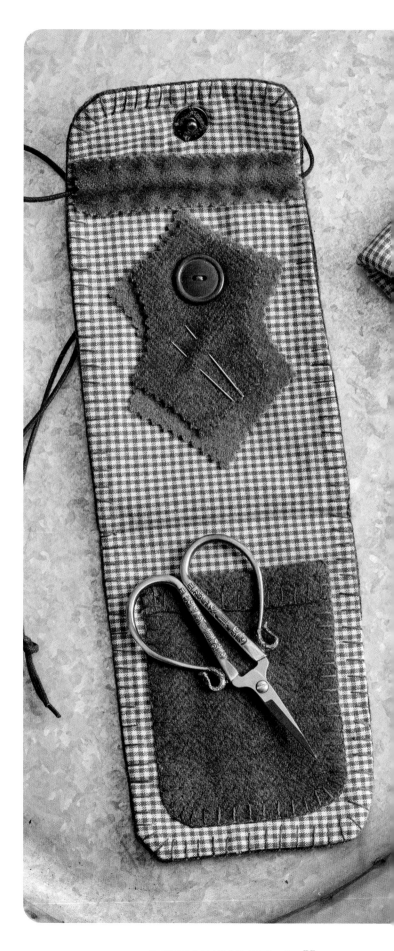

5 With right sides together, align the edges of the pouch outside and lining. Machine sew ¼" from all edges, leaving an opening for turning. Turn right side out and press flat. Using red pearl cotton, blanket-stitch along the outside edges, closing the opening.

6 Referring to the appliqué placement diagram, mark fold lines on the pouch and press. Unfold, then hand sew the snap halves to opposite ends of the pouch body and sew the red 1" button to the flap.

7 Position the red wool 1" × 4" strip over the bottom fold line and sew with a running stitch close to the long edges only. Feed the black cord through the wool strip, then tie the ends in a knot to make the strap. Use the slits to button the needle pages onto the red ¾" button inside the pouch.

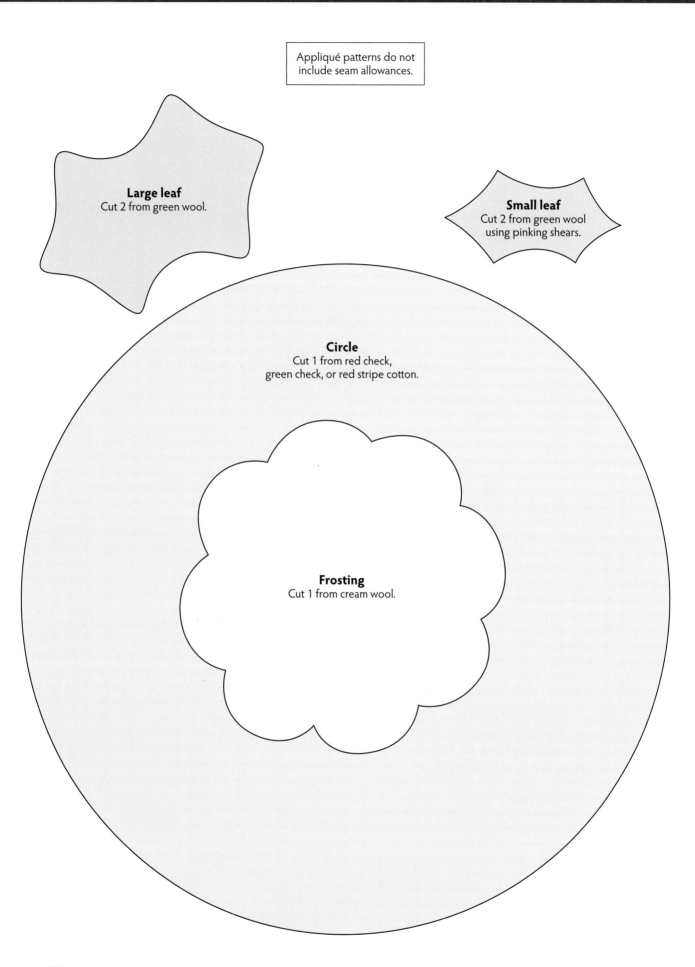

Appliqué patterns do not
include seam allowances.

Large leaf
Cut 2 from green wool.

Small leaf
Cut 2 from green wool
using pinking shears.

Circle
Cut 1 from red check,
green check, or red stripe cotton.

Frosting
Cut 1 from cream wool.

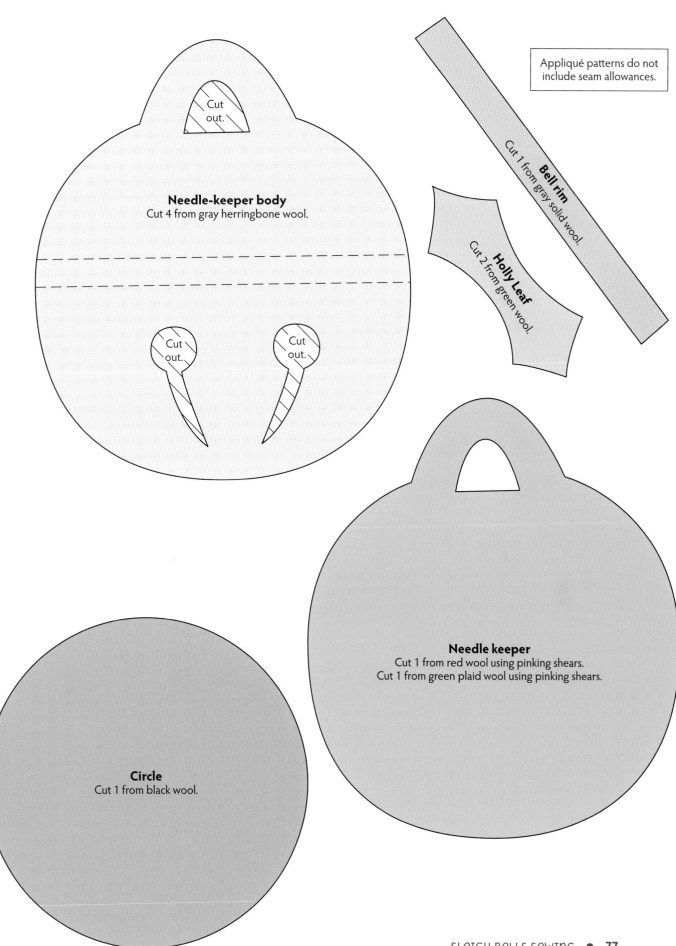

Appliqué patterns do not include seam allowances.

Bell rim
Cut 1 from gray solid wool.

Holly Leaf
Cut 2 from green wool.

Cut out.

Needle-keeper body
Cut 4 from gray herringbone wool.

Cut out.

Cut out.

Needle keeper
Cut 1 from red wool using pinking shears.
Cut 1 from green plaid wool using pinking shears.

Circle
Cut 1 from black wool.

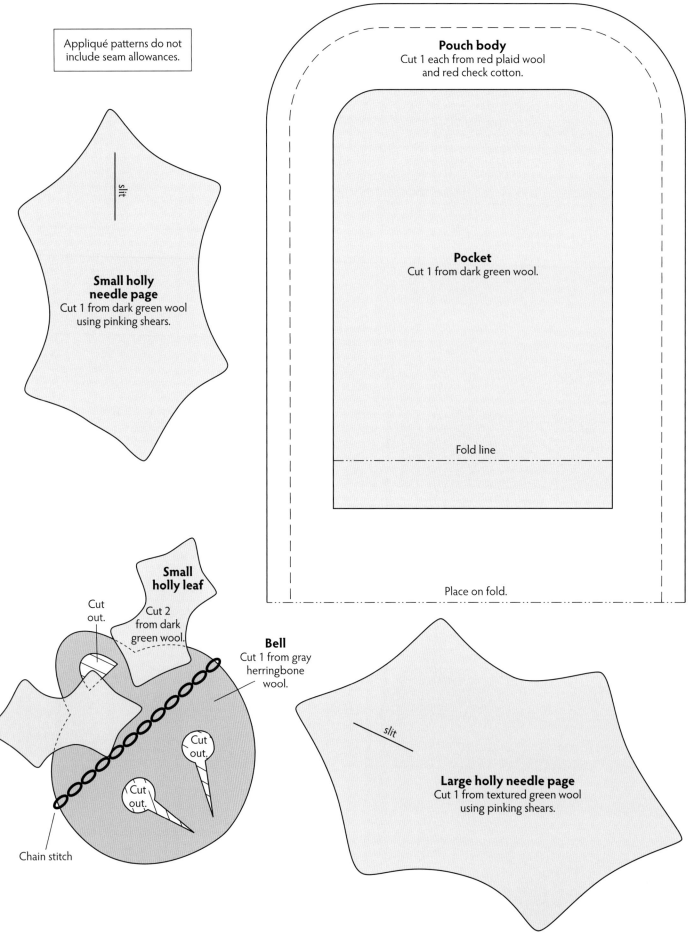

Appliqué patterns do not include seam allowances.

Small holly needle page
Cut 1 from dark green wool using pinking shears.

slit

Pouch body
Cut 1 each from red plaid wool and red check cotton.

Pocket
Cut 1 from dark green wool.

Fold line

Place on fold.

Small holly leaf
Cut 2 from dark green wool.

Cut out.

Bell
Cut 1 from gray herringbone wool.

Cut out.

Cut out.

Chain stitch

Large holly needle page
Cut 1 from textured green wool using pinking shears.

slit

Ginger and Spice

And everything nice, that's how the saying goes. When you stitch this collection of assorted bowl fillers, I think you'll agree. This baking-themed group is oh-so-nice indeed!

Merry Christmas Gingerbread Bowl Filler

FINISHED SIZE: 4½" × 6"

Materials

- × 5" × 6½" piece of tan linen for front
- × 5" × 6½" piece of tan check cotton for backing
- × 5" × 5" square of brown wool for gingerbread body
- × 1½" × 2" piece of red wool for hearts
- × 1" × 3" piece of brown plaid wool for opening closure
- × 12" length of ³⁄₁₆"-wide tan rickrack
- × 2 black buttons for eyes, ¼" diameter
- × Size 12 pearl cotton in black, brown, and tan
- × Tan sewing thread
- × Fiberfill stuffing
- × Embroidery and hand-sewing needles

Stitching and Assembly

1 Use the patterns (page 81) to cut out the gingerbread and heart appliqués.

2 Position and pin the gingerbread body in the lower-left corner of the tan linen 5½" × 6½" piece, leaving a ¼" seam allowance. Blanket-stitch around it with brown pearl cotton.

3 Position and pin the hearts in place. Whipstitch using black pearl cotton.

4 Pin the rickrack around the inside edge of the blanket stitching on the gingerbread body. Couch in place with a single strand of tan sewing thread.

Spice 'em Up!

Why not make your gingerbread bowl fillers smell as nice as a bowl full of homemade cookies? Add a few whole cloves to the stuffing to enjoy a little whiff of goodness when you handle them.

5 Sew the buttons in place for eyes. Using black pearl cotton, backstitch the mouth and make straight stitches for the eyebrows.

6 Transfer the words *Merry Christmas* onto the linen above the gingerbread body. Backstitch with brown pearl cotton. Press.

7 Referring to "Assembling Bowl Fillers and Small Pillows" (page 27), sew and stuff the pillow.

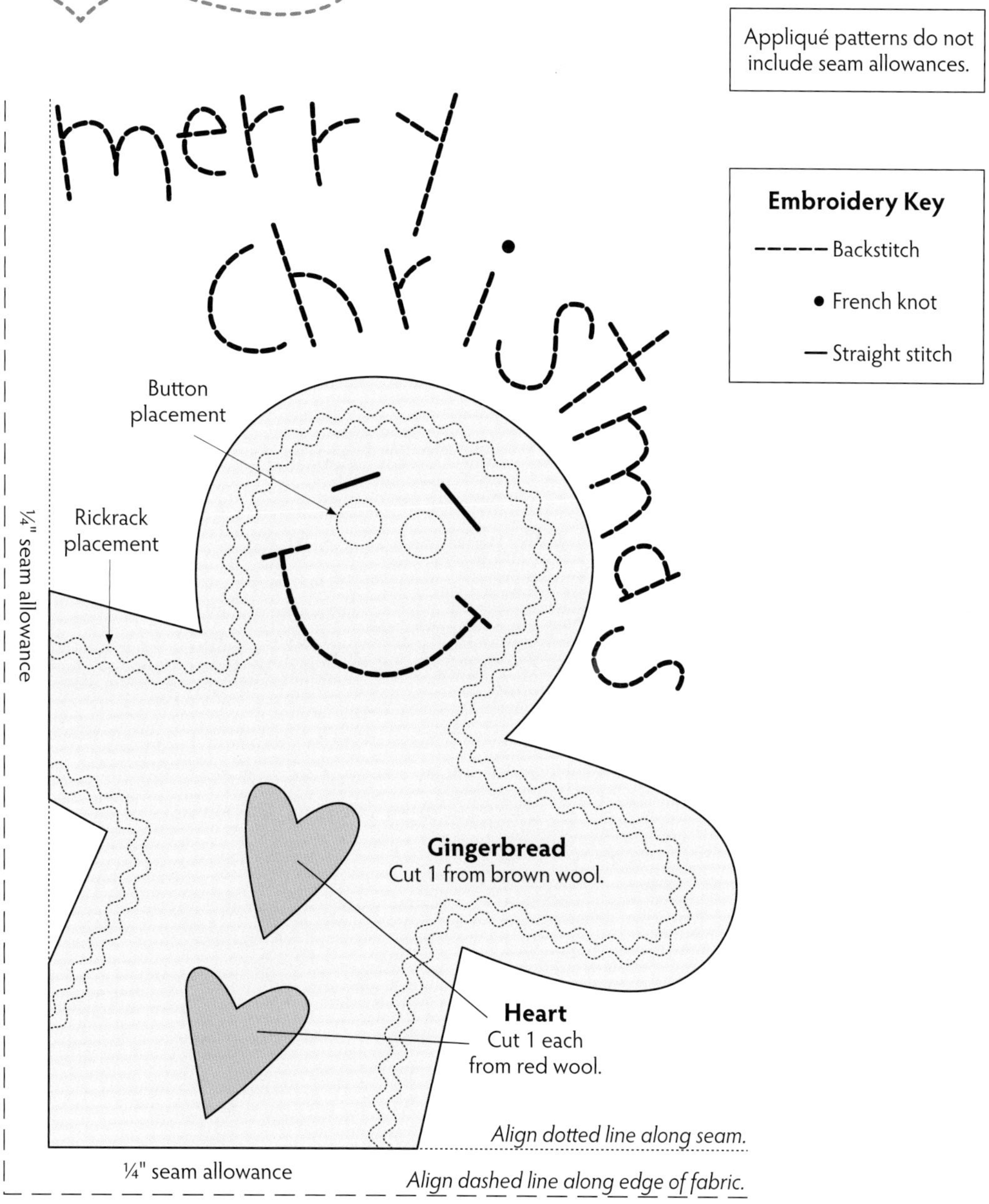

Appliqué patterns do not include seam allowances.

Embroidery Key

- - - - - Backstitch

● French knot

— Straight stitch

¼" seam allowance

Button placement

Rickrack placement

Gingerbread
Cut 1 from brown wool.

Heart
Cut 1 each from red wool.

Align dotted line along seam.

¼" seam allowance

Align dashed line along edge of fabric.

Merry Christmas Gingerbread Bowl Filler

Cookies Bowl Filler

FINISHED SIZE: 4½" × 5"

Materials

- × 4" × 5½" piece of cream cotton for front
- × 1½" × 5½" piece of brown check cotton for front
- × 5" × 5½" piece of brown wool for back
- × 6" length of ³⁄₁₆"-wide tan rickrack
- × 4 cream buttons, ½" diameter
- × Size 12 pearl cotton in black, brown, cream, green, and red
- × Tan sewing thread
- × Fiberfill stuffing
- × Embroidery and hand-sewing needles

Stitching and Assembly

Press the seam allowances as shown by the arrow.

1 Sew together the cream cotton 4" × 5½" piece and brown check 1½" × 5½" piece to make the front, which should be 5" × 5½", including seam allowances.

Make 1 front,
5" × 5½".

2 Transfer the embroidery design from the pattern (page 83) onto the pieced front.

3 Using brown pearl cotton, backstitch two lines for the gingerbread cookie outline. Using green pearl cotton, chain stitch across the neck and sew lazy daisy stitches for leaves on each side of the chain stitches. Using red pearl cotton, make five French knots along the chain stitch for berries; backstitch the heart.

4 Using black pearl cotton, embroider the word *cookies* on the gingerbread. Using cream pearl cotton, sew straight stitches across the arms and legs. Using brown pearl cotton, make cross-stitches over the top of the straight stitches on the arms and legs. Using black pearl cotton, make two French knots for eyes.

5 Sew the 6" rickrack piece down the seamline of the front using a couching stitch and tan thread.

6 Sew the four ½" cream buttons in place on the checked fabric in a row.

7 Referring to "Assembling Bowl Fillers and Small Pillows" (page 27), sew and stuff the bowl filler.

Cookies Bowl Filler

Embroidery Key

- - - - -	Backstitch
⚬⚬⚬⚬	Chain stitch
✕ ✕	Cross-stitch
•	French knot
⚬	Lazy daisy
—	Straight stitch

Plaid Gingerbread Bowl Filler

FINISHED SIZE: 4½" × 5½"

Materials

- × 5" × 6" piece of black wool for gingerbread outline
- × 4½" × 5½" piece of brown plaid wool for gingerbread
- × 2" × 2" square of green wool for holly leaves
- × 5" × 6" piece of brown check cotton for front
- × 5" × 6" piece of brown stripe cotton for back
- × ¾" × 3" piece of brown wool for opening cover
- × 1 white button, ½" diameter
- × Size 12 pearl cotton in black, brown, cream, green, and red
- × Fiberfill stuffing

Stitching and Assembly

1 Use the patterns below to cut out the gingerbread and leaf appliqués.

2 Center the gingerbread on the black wool 5" × 6" piece. Whipstitch using brown pearl cotton.

3 Using cream pearl cotton, chain stitch across the arms and legs of the gingerbread.

4 Trim the excess black wool a scant ¼" from the gingerbread. Center the gingerbread on the brown check 5" × 6" piece and whipstitch using black pearl cotton.

5 Position and pin the leaf appliqués on the gingerbread. Whipstitch using green pearl cotton.

6 Using a double strand of red pearl cotton, make five French knots for berries.

7 Sew the button in place on the body.

8 Referring to "Assembling Bowl Fillers and Small PIllows" (page 27), sew and stuff the bowl filler. Cover the closed opening with the ¾" × 3" piece of brown wool and whipstitch around the edges using matching pearl cotton. Optional: Sew a featherstitch across the ¾" × 3" wool using black pearl cotton.

> Appliqué patterns do not include seam allowances.

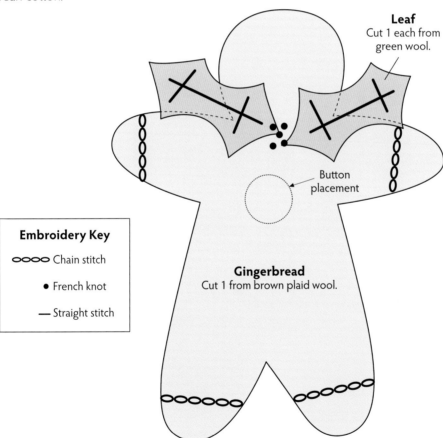

Leaf
Cut 1 each from green wool.

Button placement

Embroidery Key

∞∞∞ Chain stitch

● French knot

— Straight stitch

Gingerbread
Cut 1 from brown plaid wool.

Plaid Gingerbread Bowl Filler

Stamp Gingerbread Bowl Filler

FINISHED SIZE: 4¼" × 5"

Materials

- ✕ 4¾" × 5½" piece of tan linen for front
- ✕ 4¾" × 5½" piece of tan check cotton for back
- ✕ 3½" × 3½" square of cream wool for stamp
- ✕ 2" × 2½" piece of brown wool for gingerbread
- ✕ 3 brown buttons, ⅜" to ½" diameter
- ✕ Size 12 pearl cotton in black, brown, and cream
- ✕ Small safety pin, ¾"
- ✕ Tiny heart charm
- ✕ Tan sewing thread
- ✕ Fiberfill stuffing

Appliqué patterns do not include seam allowances.

Embroidery Key

––––– Backstitch

• French knot

Stitching and Assembly

1 Use the patterns below to cut out the gingerbread and stamp appliqués.

2 Transfer the word *gingerbread* onto the tan linen 4¾" × 5½" piece and backstitch the letters using black pearl cotton. Make a French knot to dot the letter *i*.

3 Position and pin the appliqués on the tan linen piece. Whipstitch using coordinating pearl cotton.

4 Using brown pearl cotton, backstitch a rectangular outline around the inside edge of the stamp.

5 Using tan sewing thread, sew a backstitch around the inside edge of the gingerbread body.

6 Sew the buttons in place above the stamp.

7 Referring to "Assembling Bowl Fillers and Small Pillows" (page 27), sew and stuff the bowl filler.

8 Using the safety pin, pin the heart charm to the stamp.

Button placement

Stamp
Cut 1 from cream wool.

Gingerbread
Cut 1 from brown wool.

Stamp Gingerbread Bowl Filler

Here Comes Santa

Back in the day, articulated toys with pull strings (often called jumping jacks) were quite popular. Stitch a nod to the past with these clever wool versions including Santa, one of his elves, and a dapper gingerbread man.

Catch Me If You Can! Ornament

FINISHED SIZE: 5½" × 7"

Materials

- 2 pieces, 8" × 9", of black wool for body outline and back
- 6" × 7" piece of brown wool for gingerbread body
- 3½" × 3½" square of brown plaid wool for vest and vest placket
- 2" × 4" piece of red wool for hearts
- 1½" × 2½" piece of green wool for bow
- 5 black buttons for vest and knees, ³⁄₁₆" diameter
- 2 black buttons for eyes, ⅛" diameter
- 10" length of cream wool yarn for hanger and pull cord
- Size 12 pearl cotton in black, brown, cream, green, and red
- Embroidery and hand-sewing needles

Stitching and Assembly

1 Use the patterns (page 89) to cut the gingerbread body, vest, vest placket, heart, and bow appliqués from wool as directed.

2 Referring to the appliqué placement diagram on page 88, position and pin the body and thighs on one black wool 8" × 9" piece, tucking the upper edges of the thighs under the bottom edge of the body piece. Position the leg pieces in place, lapping the top edge of the legs over the thighs. Blanket-stitch around all pieces with brown pearl cotton.

Appliqué placement

3 Position and pin the vest in place on the gingerbread body and blanket-stitch around the edges using brown pearl cotton. Pin the vest placket in place and whipstitch around the edges using brown pearl cotton.

4 Position and whipstitch the small red heart in place on the vest using red pearl cotton.

5 Position and pin the green bow in place. Blanket-stitch around the edges using green pearl cotton. Backstitch along the inside edge of the blanket stitching. Using a double strand of green pearl cotton, sew a lazy daisy stitch in the center of each side of the bow for leaves. Using a double strand of red pearl cotton, make three French knots in the center for berries.

6 Using cream pearl cotton, sew straight stitches across the ends of the arms and feet and then use a couching stitch to pull the stitches into a zigzag formation.

Creative Embellishments

Consider using tiny rickrack on the gingerbread man's arms and legs, a red heart button, and a ribbon to make his bow tie. Find a small brass buckle to use for Santa's belt, and couch white chenille yarn to fluff up his cuffs and hat brim.

7 Using cream pearl cotton, make a zigzag design around the head using straight stitches. Sew buttons in place for eyes. Using black pearl cotton, backstitch and straight stitch the eyebrows and mouth.

8 Using red pearl cotton, make cheeks with a star stitch.

9 Sew the buttons in place on the gingerbread knees and on the vest placket.

10 Cut away the excess black wool to ¼" from the edge of the gingerbread body. Position and pin the front onto the remaining black wool 8" × 9" piece. Trim the black wool piece even with the edges of the front. Using black pearl cotton, blanket-stitch around the edges, joining the front and back pieces.

11 Place the two large red hearts together and blanket-stitch around the edges using red pearl cotton.

12 Cut the wool yarn in half to make two 5" lengths. Thread one length through the bottom center of the body and to the top of the large red heart, tying a knot at each end. Make a hanger with the remaining length by threading it through the top of the head and tying a loop.

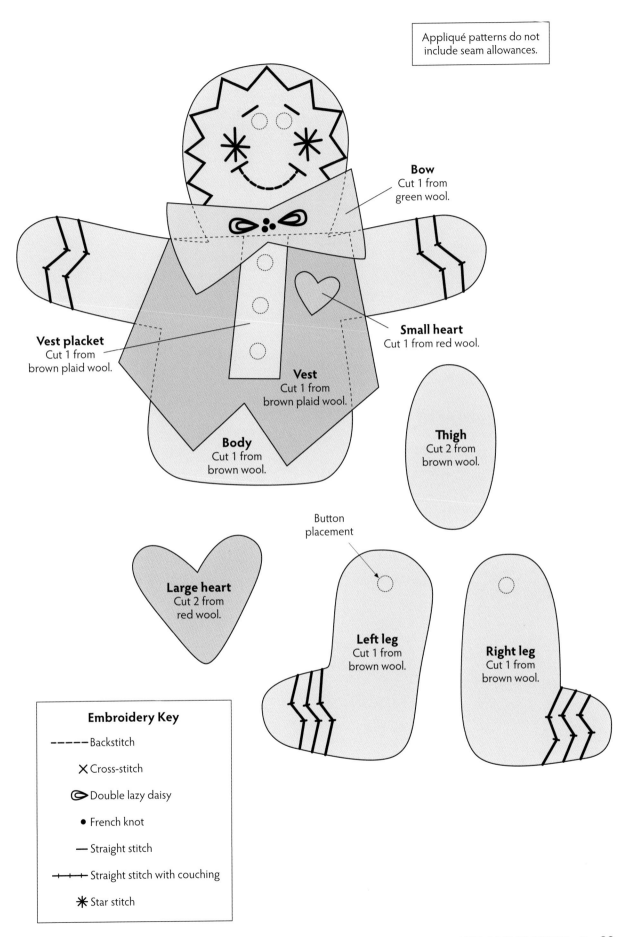

Appliqué patterns do not include seam allowances.

Bow
Cut 1 from green wool.

Small heart
Cut 1 from red wool.

Vest placket
Cut 1 from brown plaid wool.

Vest
Cut 1 from brown plaid wool.

Thigh
Cut 2 from brown wool.

Body
Cut 1 from brown wool.

Large heart
Cut 2 from red wool.

Button placement

Left leg
Cut 1 from brown wool.

Right leg
Cut 1 from brown wool.

Embroidery Key

- - - - - Backstitch

✕ Cross-stitch

🌀 Double lazy daisy

● French knot

— Straight stitch

+++++ Straight stitch with couching

✳ Star stitch

Santa's Elf Ornament

FINISHED SIZE: 6½" × 8"

Materials

× 2 pieces, 8" × 10", of black wool for elf body outline and back

× 3" × 6" piece of green wool for shirt, arms, and hat

× 3" × 4" piece of solid red wool for collar, mittens, and hatband

× 2" × 4" piece of red striped wool for legs (make sure stripe goes horizontally)

× 2" × 2½" piece of flesh wool for face

× 1" × 2" piece of light brown wool for hair

× 2" × 4" piece of medium brown wool for boots

× 4 black buttons for legs and knees, ¼" diameter

× Embroidery floss in black, brown, flesh, green, and red

× Size 12 pearl cotton in black

× 5 mini bells for collar, ¼" diameter

× 1 medium bell for hat, ½" diameter

× 30" length of black jute for hanger and bows

Stitching and Assembly

1 Use the patterns (page 91) to cut the shirt, arms, hat, collar, mittens, hatband, legs, face, nose, boots, and hair appliqués from wool as directed.

2 Referring to the appliqué placement diagram, position and pin all of the appliqué pieces on one black wool 8" × 10" piece. Whipstitch around all pieces with one strand of coordinating embroidery floss. Press.

Appliqué placement

3 Backstitch the mouth using a single strand of black embroidery floss. Make French knots for the eyes using a double strand of black embroidery floss.

4 Cut away the excess black wool to ¼" from the edge of the appliqué pieces. Position and pin the front onto the remaining black wool 8" × 10" piece. Trim the black wool piece even with the edges of the front. Using black pearl cotton, blanket-stitch around the edges, joining the front and back pieces.

5 Sew the black ¼" buttons in place on the legs and knees.

6 Sew the five small bells in place at each collar point. Sew the medium bell at the top of the hat.

7 Thread an 8" piece of black jute through the top of the hat and tie in a knot for a hanger.

8 Cut the remaining jute into five equal pieces. Tie each piece into a bow and tack them on the boots, mittens, and hat.

Appliqué patterns do not include seam allowances.

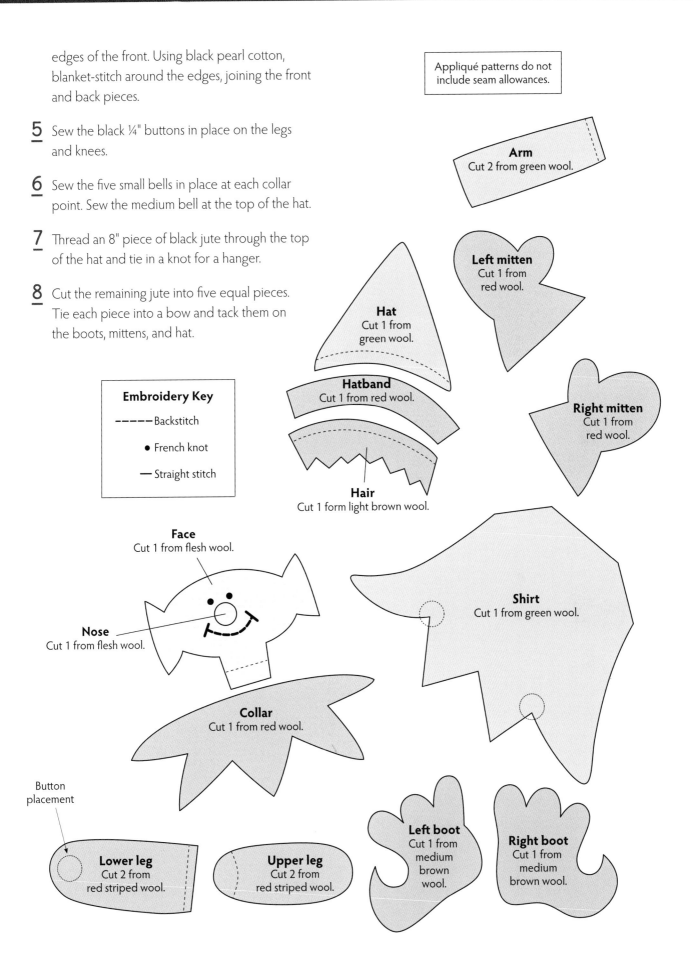

Arm
Cut 2 from green wool.

Left mitten
Cut 1 from red wool.

Hat
Cut 1 from green wool.

Right mitten
Cut 1 from red wool.

Embroidery Key

----- Backstitch

• French knot

— Straight stitch

Hatband
Cut 1 from red wool.

Hair
Cut 1 form light brown wool.

Face
Cut 1 from flesh wool.

Nose
Cut 1 from flesh wool.

Shirt
Cut 1 from green wool.

Collar
Cut 1 from red wool.

Button placement

Lower leg
Cut 2 from red striped wool.

Upper leg
Cut 2 from red striped wool.

Left boot
Cut 1 from medium brown wool.

Right boot
Cut 1 from medium brown wool.

Jumping-Jack Santa
FINISHED SIZE: 9" × 12"

Materials

- ✕ 2 pieces, 10" × 13", of black wool for body outline and back
- ✕ 7" × 7" square of red plaid wool for Santa shirt and arms
- ✕ 6" × 6" square of white wool for beard, mustache, hatband, bobble, cuffs, and shirt border
- ✕ 3" × 7" piece of red wool for legs, nose, and hat
- ✕ 2" × 3½" piece of gray wool for mittens
- ✕ 1" × 2" piece of cream wool for face
- ✕ 2" × 2" square of gold wool for belt buckle
- ✕ 2½" × 5" piece of black wool for boots and belt
- ✕ 2 black buttons for elbows, ½" diameter
- ✕ 2 black buttons for knees, ⅜" diameter

- ✕ 5 cream buttons for shirt border and pull, ½" to ⅝" diameter
- ✕ Size 12 pearl cotton in black, cream, gold, gray, and red
- ✕ 15" length of cream wool yarn for hanger and pull

Stitching and Assembly

1 Use the patterns (page 93-94) to cut the shirt, arm, beard, mustache, hatband, bobble, cuff, shirt border, leg, hat, mitten, face, belt buckle, and boot appliqués from wool as directed.

2 Referring to the appliqué placement diagram, position and pin all of the appliqué pieces in 10 different sections on one black wool 10" × 13" piece. Whipstitch around all pieces with coordinating pearl cotton. Press.

Appliqué placement 1

3 For the head unit, use cream pearl cotton to backstitch around the inside of the whipstitching on the beard, mustache, and hat bobble. Sew a French knot in the center of the hat bobble and throughout the beard. Sew cross-stitches across the hatband. Using black pearl cotton, make two French knots for eyes.

4 For the middle unit, use gold pearl cotton to stitch French knots in the middle portion of the buckle. Using cream pearl cotton, featherstitch a line across the border on the shirt. Sew four cream buttons to the border.

5 For the lower-arm units, use cream pearl cotton to make four cross-stitches across the sleeve cuffs.

6 For the lower-leg units, use cream pearl cotton to make four cross-stitches across the pant cuffs.

7 On each of the 10 sections, cut away the excess black wool to ¼" from the edge of the appliqué pieces. Position and pin the pieces onto the remaining black wool 10" × 13" piece. Trim the black wool piece even with the edges of the front. Using black pearl cotton, blanket-stitch around the edges, joining the front and back pieces. Press.

8 Join the Santa sections by sewing them together with black pearl cotton. Sew the black buttons in place on the elbows and knees.

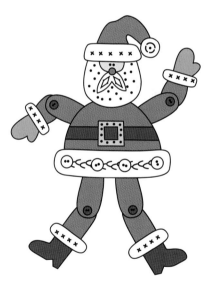

Appliqué placement 2

9 Cut the wool yarn in half. Sew one length through the top of the hat and tie in a knot for a hanger. Tie the other length to the remaining cream button and sew the other end to the bottom of the coat to make him a jumping-jack Santa.

Appliqué patterns do not include seam allowances.

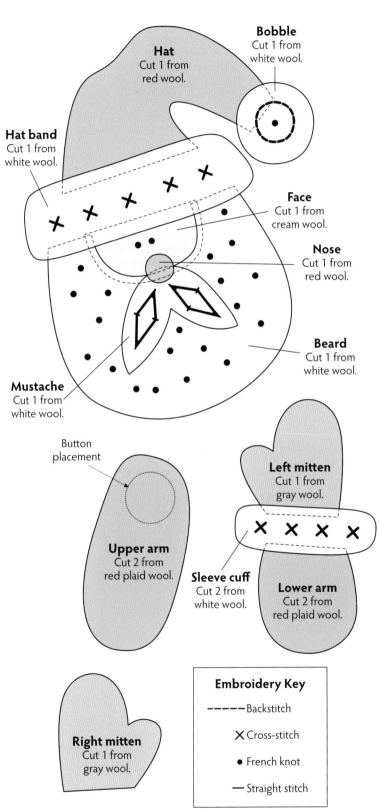

Hat
Cut 1 from red wool.

Bobble
Cut 1 from white wool.

Hat band
Cut 1 from white wool.

Face
Cut 1 from cream wool.

Nose
Cut 1 from red wool.

Beard
Cut 1 from white wool.

Mustache
Cut 1 from white wool.

Button placement

Upper arm
Cut 2 from red plaid wool.

Sleeve cuff
Cut 2 from white wool.

Left mitten
Cut 1 from gray wool.

Lower arm
Cut 2 from red plaid wool.

Right mitten
Cut 1 from gray wool.

Embroidery Key

----- Backstitch

X Cross-stitch

• French knot

— Straight stitch

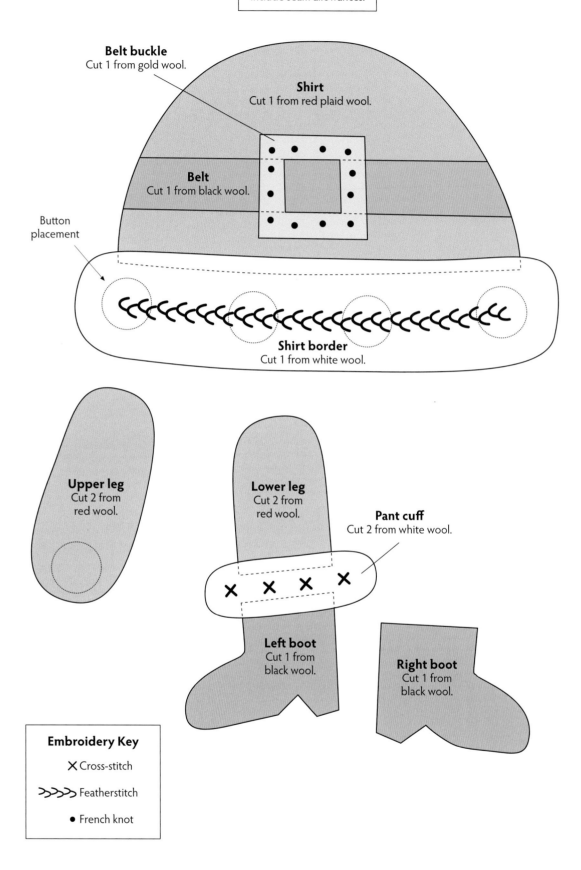

Appliqué patterns do not include seam allowances.

Belt buckle
Cut 1 from gold wool.

Shirt
Cut 1 from red plaid wool.

Belt
Cut 1 from black wool.

Button placement

Shirt border
Cut 1 from white wool.

Upper leg
Cut 2 from red wool.

Lower leg
Cut 2 from red wool.

Pant cuff
Cut 2 from white wool.

Left boot
Cut 1 from black wool.

Right boot
Cut 1 from black wool.

Embroidery Key

X Cross-stitch

>>>> Featherstitch

• French knot

Resources

Blackberry Primitives
Lincoln, Nebraska
www.blackberryprimitives.com
Wool

Diamond Textiles
Pacoima, California
www.diamondtextilesusa.com
Wholesale woven fabrics

Heavens to Betsy
Claverack, New York
www.heavens-to-betsy.com
Wool

Just Another Button Company
Troy, Illinois
www.justanotherbuttoncompany.com
Handmade and hand-dyed buttons

Valdani
www.valdani.com
Pearl cotton and floss

Wooden Spool Designs
www.woodenspooldesigns.com
Patterns

Acknowledgments

Thank you seems never enough:

Jeff Busby, for your never-ending love, patience, and encouragement over so many years. Without you I could not do what I love to do: stitch!

My priceless children, Ivo, Amy, Daniel, and Karah, for your constant support and love.

To my beautiful grandchildren, Addison, Hailey, Emma, Olivia, Lincoln, Hazel, Xy, and Thea, for always thinking that whatever I create is awesome!

Thank you to my very special publishing team for inviting me to write this book to share my love for hand stitching with so many others!

About the Author

I grew up in three states in the Pacific Northwest: Oregon, Washington, and Idaho (in the city of Star, where I currently live). Being married to my best friend, Jeff Busby, for 45 years is what keeps me in stitches! When we married in 1976, our very first purchase was a Kenmore sewing machine from Sears, Roebuck and Co. Those first 10 years I cranked out a lot of clothes for myself to help us save money on apparel and then moved on to sewing clothes for my children, matching outfits for the cousins, and Christmas gifts for family and friends.

After the kids were past the age that they would wear homemade clothes, I moved on to sewing crafts to sell at craft fairs with my mom. She was a great encouragement and cheerleader to me during that time. We would sew like crazy, attend a craft fair, sell out, and sew like crazy again for the next one. I mostly made dolls and worked with cotton back then, which included a lot of cotton-fused appliqué and blanket-stitched appliqué work.

I began sewing shop samples for several local quilt shops, which led to my introduction to wool appliqué back in the mid-1990s. As time passes, so do those we love, and toward the end of my mother's struggle with cancer, she encouraged me to try designing a pattern of my own. She passed in 2001, and keeping my promise to her, I've been designing with wool since 2002.

I have had the privilege of traveling throughout the states and into Australia to teach and vend, meeting so many wonderfully kind and talented people across the country whose passion is hand stitching. I love to teach others about wool and see them enjoy its simplicity and rewards.

When I'm not stitching, designing patterns and fabric, teaching, or vending for my business, Wooden Spool Designs, I love to garden, go to the beach, and spend time with my eight grandchildren. My future dream is to pass on to them the art of being creative in whatever they do.